MW01252910

Demystifying the Chinese Miracle

The last three decades has witnessed miraculous economic growth of China. What has accounted for its miracle? What is the nature and future of the Chinese model? Is it unique?

This book presents an analytical framework to demystify China's economic growth miracle. The book suggests that interlinked and relational contracts between the agents (in particular, between the state and the business) can compensate for flawed markets to achieve high growth. This kind of relational capitalism is significant in the investment-based stage of development, when mobilization of resources to exploit the existing technologies is the key for growth.

The book presents a general theory of the interlinked relational contract, the workhorse model of the book. The theory highlights that effective governance is a function of market extent and market completeness. The process of economic development and modernization can be looked at fruitfully from two perspectives: the markets and the institutions; and their interactions. The book stresses the critical fit between the development stage and the governance for a country's economic transition and development and thus the idea of "appropriate institutions".

Yongqin Wang is currently Associate Professor at the China Center for Economic Studies (CCES), Fudan University, China, and has held a visiting position at Yale University (2008–2010). He received his PhD in Economics from Fudan University in 2004 and has also attended Queen's University (Kingston, Canada) and IDEI, University of Toulouse 1 (Toulouse, France) as a visiting scholar. His main research interests include microeconomic theory, financial economics, development economics, and Chinese economy.

Routledge Studies in the Modern World Economy

Demystifying the Chinese Miracle

The rise and future of
relational capitalism

Yongqin Wang

Routledge
Taylor & Francis Group

LONDON AND NEW YORK

First published 2014
by Routledge
2 Park Square, Milton Park, Abingdon, Oxon, OX14 4RN

Simultaneously published in the USA and Canada
by Routledge
711 Third Avenue, New York, NY 10017

Routledge is an imprint of the Taylor & Francis Group, an informa business

This book has been sponsored by the Chinese Fund for the Humanities
and Social Sciences

British Library Cataloguing in Publication Data
A catalogue record for this book is available from the British Library

Library of Congress Cataloging in Publication Data
Wang, Yongqin.
Demystifying the Chinese miracle : the rise and future of relational
capitalism / by Yongqin Wang.
  pages cm. – (Routledge studies in the modern world economy ; 117)
Includes bibliographical references and index.
1. China–Economic conditions–2000– 2. Organizational
change–China–History–21st century. I. Title.
HC427.95.W3682 2013
330.951–dc23   2013000365

ISBN: 978-0-415-68107-0 (hbk)
ISBN: 978-0-203-75452-8 (ebk)

Typeset in Times New Roman
By Deer Park Productions

Contents

Figures and tables

Figures

Tables

Acknowledgements

This book is an outgrowth of my Chinese version book, *The Great Transformation: Interlinked Relational Contracts and China's Miracle*, published by Truth & Wisdom Press, and articles published in Chinese and English journals, including *Journal of Chinese Political Science*, *Transition Studies Review*, *Studies in Regional Development*, *Economic Research Journal* (Chinese), *Management World* (Chinese), and *World Economic Papers* (Chinese). I am grateful to the editors of the Chinese book and the articles, for their early input in editing and allowing me to incorporate the ideas in the current book, in particular Yuanlong He and Na Li. Some chapters are based on my collaborations with my co-authors, including Te Bao, Ming Li and Ming Lu. I appreciate their input very much. The English version has been based on a first draft of translation by Feng Xue, and proofread by Matthew Hummer, Thomas K. Mehaffy and Peter Zeitz. Thanks also go to numerous colleagues who have provided insightful comments along the way and whose names are too many to enumerate here.

The research project for this book has been sponsored by the Chinese Fund for Humanities and Social Sciences, Shanghai Pujiang Program, Program for New Century Excellent Talents in University (NCET), Project 985 of Fudan University, China Social Science Foundation Project (05CJL014), Fudan Lab for China Development Studies the MOE Project of the Key Research Institute of Humanities and Social Sciences at Universities (07JJD790130) and Shanghai Leading Academic Discipline Project (B101); all these are gratefully acknowledged.

Last but not least, the unlimited support from my beloved family, especially my wife Na Li and my parents, has been essential to this book. They have suffered from my preoccupation with the manuscript during the time of writing. I dedicate this book to them.

1   Introduction

Motivations and questions

The last three decades have witnessed China's history-making economic growth, with an average annual growth rate of over 9 percent, despite a general lacking of sound legal system, financial system and other formal institutions. From an international perspective, China's transition so far is undoubtedly a huge success when compared either with other transition economies like Russia, or with any other developing economy. It is an intriguing challenge for social scientists to offer some theory to account for the economic miracle and to predict its future.

China's current growth record is reminiscent of those of the East Asia developmental states after World War II, which had comparable growth records. Japan, and later, four industrialized economies – Korea, Taiwan, Singapore and Hong Kong – had comparable annual growth rate for almost three decades. Now these economies are all high-income developed economies. During their catch-up period, most of these economies share the following features. (1) Authoritarian governments played a substantial role in economic development through various policy instruments, like industrial policy. (2) The role of the legal system was not that pervasive, as in the Western world, while relational contracting played an important role in socioeconomic life. (3) The economic structure was centralized and there were a few big firms and banks as major players in economic arena. There is long-term relationship between banks and firms, and banks are dominant financing sources for large corporations. (4) Economic success at preliminary stages, once dubbed as Asia's miracle, was followed by economic crisis in many economies at the end of 1990s. Japan, for instance, began to fall into long-term stagnation even in the early 1990s. (5) From the perspective of political transformation, the free market system was accompanied by a political democratization process in these economies. What's behind the East Asian miracle? Are there similarities between the East Asian miracle and the Chinese miracle?

Conventional wisdom suggests the protection of private property, a sound legal system, government transparency and an efficient financial system contribute

Table 1.1 The rule of law index

Country/Region	2004	2002	2000	1998	1996
Singapore	95.7	92.3	98.9	99.5	99.4
Hong Kong	90.3	84.7	90.4	90.8	90.4
Japan	89.9	88.3	90.9	90.3	88.0
Hungary	78.7	77.6	78.6	76.2	75.3
South Korea	68.6	76.5	73.8	76.8	81.9
Malaysia	64.7	67.9	71.1	76.8	82.5
Turkey	54.6	53.1	59.9	65.9	58.4
Thailand	51.7	60.2	69.0	69.2	71.1
India	50.7	55.6	62.0	67.0	56.6
Romania	48.3	52.0	51.9	49.7	44.0
Brazil	46.9	45.9	53.5	56.8	46.4
Mexico	45.9	47.4	46.0	40.0	54.2
China	*40.6*	*48.5*	*48.7*	*52.4*	*37.3*
Peru	31.9	36.7	38.5	37.3	40.4
Russia	29.5	21.4	18.7	22.7	19.9
Ukraine	23.2	21.4	26.2	23.2	28.3

Note: From 0 to 100, the higher the score, the better the rule of law.

Source: Kaufmann *et al.* (2005).

to economic development. Interestingly, there were weak formal institutions in place during China's transition. Table 1.1 shows that the rule of law index is rather low for China. In historical retrospect, authoritarian governments played a pivotal role in economic development at the early stages of economic takeoff in East Asia. In the past 30 years international organizations like the World Bank and the IMF have made futile attempts to introduce a set of standard formal institutions (the so-called "Washington Consensus") in the developing world. A general question thus arises: what is the relationship between institutions and economic development?

This book presents a theoretical framework to account for the dynamic relationship between economic development and institutions. The basic idea is as follows. The efficient institution is a function of the extent of market and the division of labor. In the stage with limited market extent and low level of specialization (incomplete market), the contracting between agents often takes the form of an interlinked relational contract, which internalizes externalities. From the perspective of the relationship between state and economic development, a government with a high level of autonomy[1] and state capacity is more likely to foster economic development through interlinked relational policies, to address the missing markets problem. In this sense, the form and extent of economic organization and government intervention is a function of economic development stages. At stages with a large extent of market and relatively complete markets, formal institutions enforced by a third party will play more important roles.

Contributions and conclusions

The extent of the market and division of labor endogenously determines the efficient forms of contract. The key to understanding the relationship between formal institutions and informal institutions is to know how economic development endogenously changes the form of contract. A theory of inter-linked relational contracts is introduced for understanding the relation between economic development and endogenous institutions. The theory shows that in a developing economy with limited extent of market and division of labor (missing markets), transactions between agents tend to be multiplex and interlinked. A typical case is share tenancy in agriculture. In a developing economy, landlord and tenant make transactions not only on the product market (tenants may buy agricultural produce from landlords), but also interact on the labor market (landlords employ tenants), the credit market (landlords provide loan to tenants), and the insurance market (through sharecropping). Thus an unprofitable contract on a separate market may be viable in an interlinked transaction. That is, the interlinking markets expand the feasible set of viable relational contracts. In an economy with more complete markets, economic transactions occur on different specialized markets among anonymous traders. Further, the interlinked and relational contract may endogenously determine the structures of economic organization and forms of property rights.

Economic development and institutional change. Economic development often unravels the interlinked relational contract through specialization and market thickness effects. With a larger extent of market and division of labor, transactions through interlinked relational contracts can now be undertaken on specialized markets. Moreover, frequency and volume of transactions made on specialized markets will be higher – that is, markets are getting "thicker" – reducing the search cost for trading partners and unraveling relational transactions. Through the two effects personal transactions are gradually giving way to impersonal transactions.

Both relation-based governance and rule-based governance can be self-sustaining. Economic development does not necessarily lead to transformation from relation-based governance into rule-based governance. The reason is that both relation-based society and rule-based society are self-sustaining. If interlinked relational transactions between agents are sufficient to suppress impersonal specialized markets and formal institutions, we may expect a relation-based society. Only when specialization effect and market thickness effect are powerful enough to unravel the viability of interlinked relational transactions, will transformation from relation-based governance into rule-based governance occur. In particular, economic history has suggested that a successful transformation usually involves both economic and political liberalization.

The role of government is a function of the stages of economic development. Government can play an important role at the early stages of economic development. At the stage of limited market extent and missing markets, inter-linked institutional arrangements (e.g. industrial policies) between government and entrepreneurs (and/or other social groups) can work as transitional substitutes for markets.

From the perspective of transaction cost, the self-enforcing relational contract is an economizing device since it involves no set-up cost for formal institutions. Thus, for early stages of economic development, this relational contract is an "appropriate institution". However, with further economic development and completing of markets, the diseconomy of the relational contract will emerge, while the formal institutions can enjoy economy of scale.

From the perspective of production technology, at the early stage of economic development, the prevailing technology is far from the world technology possibility frontier. So it is sufficient to use available mature technology. The key to economic growth is how to mobilize and organize resources effectively. Stable relational contracts are especially helpful for this investment-based growth stage. In contrast, later at the innovation-based growth stage where the prevailing technology is on the world frontier, rule-based governance (formal institution) is more conducive to endogenous technological progress since it has more economy of scale.

The role of the rule of law is also a function of the economic development stage. At the early stages of economic development, effective governance often takes the form of self-sustaining interlinked relational contracts and the role of the rule of law is limited for the following reasons. With interlinked relational contracts, when making decisions agents are forward-looking, taking account of future periods. In contrast, legal judgments are often backward-looking. Moreover, since the transactions are interlinked, legal judgments cannot always take into account the complex contractual interlinkage. Given all this, agents may choose not to go to court. Only when markets are sufficiently complete with economic development will the rule of law play a more significant role.

Timing and sequencing for economic liberalization. At the early stages of economic development, a centralized economic system and barriers to entry are conducive to long-term investment. But when it comes to the innovation-based growth stage, monopolized market structures restrict free entry and undermine technological innovation and future economic development. Thus economic liberalization should involve transforming the centralized structure into a decentralized one. Due to the interlinking of markets, sequencing of economic liberalizations matters for successful transition.

Timing for democratization and rule of law. The interlinked relational contract is an appropriate institution for early stages of economic development. At a certain point in the process of economic development, democratization and the rule of law are needed to lay the institutional foundation for the transformation from a relation-based society into a rule-based society. Democratization and the rule of law are usually accompanied by economic liberalization. In addition, history tells us that equality in initial endowments is essential to solid democratization and the rule of law.

The watershed between traditional society and modern society. In traditional society people interact on the basis of interlinked relational contracts due to missing markets and limited market extent. The traditional society is characterized by a multiplex relationship and simple economic structure. In contrast, there is single interest and complex economic structure in modern society. In traditional society, economic relationships are embedded in social relationships and political relationships, while in modern society, economic relationships are relatively independent of social and political relationships.

Understanding China's economic transition. The transition from a planned economy to a market economy is an unprecedented large-scale institutional change. Market incompleteness and imperfections common at early stages of transition call for institutional arrangements for economic development different from those in developed market economies. This difference is reflected in the role of government, the form of property rights and economic organizations. Given market incompleteness imperfections, interaction between government and agents endogenously determines the form of property rights and other institutional arrangements. The way the government and agents interact affects the economic performance and development trajectories.

In this regard China's gradual transition so far has been successful to the extent that the government with high autonomy and state capability interacts with enterprises (and other agents) through interlinked relational contracts, making up for missing markets. With completion of markets a transformation from relation-based society to a rule-based society is essential for further economic growth.

Understanding the East Asia model. During early stages of development in East Asia, interlinked relational contracts have played an important role in socioeconomic life as an effective substitute for missing markets. It is a more cost-effective governance structure than formal contracts at this investment-based growth stage.

The economy was monopolized by a few big firms at the early stages of development in East Asia. Monopoly and oligopoly form an effective market structure under relational contracts in the sense that relational contracts can be sustained by long-term relationships among a limited number of fixed agents. Monopoly and barriers to entry are essential to the sustainability of relational contracts. During the investment-based growth period, this sort of stable relationship is beneficial to economic development. But later on, when economic growth is based on innovation, monopoly and barriers to entry will undermine growth by harming endogenous technological progress.

A general lesson we may draw from the East Asia model is that the role of government is contingent on the stage of economic development. At early stages of economic development, the government adopts a series of policies to foster economic development in the absence of specialized markets. When the market system is in place, the government should withdraw from intensive interventions and focus on creating a level field for competition.

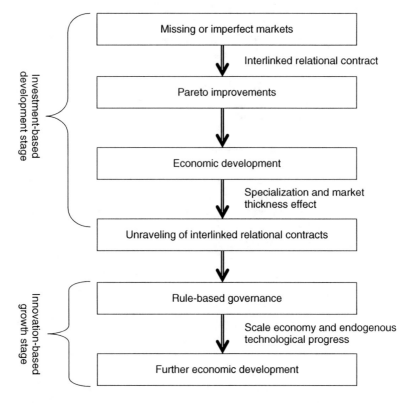

Figure 1.1 The relationship between economic development and institutional changes.

The relationship discussed here between economic development and institutions can be summarized in Figure 1.1.

Structure of the book

Chapter 2 presents the theory of the interlinked relational contract, the workhorse model of the book. The theory shows that effective governance is a function of market extent and the degree of division of labor (market completeness). The process of economic development and modernization can be looked at from two perspectives. From the perspective of the market it is a transformation from interlinked "markets" to specialized markets. From the perspective of the institution, it is a transformation from a self-enforcing interlinked relational contract toward a formal contract enforced by a third party. The match between development stage and governance matters a lot for economic transition and development.

Chapter 3 explicitly models economic growth and contract form and simulates the process of market extension and economic growth. Chapter 4 is a review of the existing theories of the interlinked contract. This chapter acts as a literature background for the book. Chapter 5 unravels China's economic miracle in light of the theory introduced in Chapter 2. Chapter 6 analyzes the East Asia model from the perspective of the interlinked relational contract and discusses its general implications for economic development and institutional change. Chapter 7 is a full account of the benefits and costs of the relational contract in China's economic transition and shows China's road to modernization.

2 Interlinking markets, relational contracts and economic transition

The transition of planned economies into market economies since the late 1980s is a remarkable historic event of large-scale institutional evolution, which has far-reaching influences on human history, providing unprecedented research opportunities for economists, sociologists and scholars in other fields. Although there is a stark contrast between the economic influences of Russian-style radical reforms and Chinese-style gradualism, with the former contributing to a sharp decrease in GDP and the latter above 9 percent annual growth rate, some economists such as Sachs, Woo and Yang (2000) still have doubts about gradual reforms. They contend that Chinese-style reforms are "partial equilibrium" reforms, which happen only in economic arenas, and thus cannot be sustainable. In contrast, the Russian-style reforms are "general equilibrium" ones, that occur in multiple arenas, and will therefore be more competitive in the long run.

Indeed, at the start of the transition process most economists supported this "Washington Consensus", which was based on neoclassical economics. As the contrast between Chinese and Russian economic performance has became clearer with time, more and more economists are arguing in favor of gradualism. Although voices favoring gradual reforms grow louder, there are still microeconomic governance mysteries that lie undiscovered behind the success of the gradual approach. The question we must first address is what microeconomic governance mechanisms assure the early successes seen under gradualism. How do such microeconomic governance mechanisms constrain further development of gradual reforms? In other words, to fully understand the cost and benefit of gradual reforms, one should first investigate microeconomic governance mechanisms underlying the gradual process.

A widely accepted viewpoint about Russian-style radical reforms and Chinese-style gradualism derives from decentralization theories based on the new Soft Budget Constraint Theory described by Dewatripont and Maskin (1995), and from interpretations based on theories of Multi-division Organization Structure and Unitary Organizational Structure (hereafter "Multi-division"). Papers along these lines include those by Qian (1994), Qian and Roland (1998), Qian, Roland and Xu (1988, 1999) and Qian and Weingast (1996). This line of literature holds that economic structures such as the degree of decentralization and the organizational structure of the entire economy account for the large gap between the economic results of reforms in China and Russia. Reforms in fiscal decentralization harden central government budget constraints of state-owned companies and also boost competition between different jurisdictional areas. Multi-division economic structure allows local institutional experiments in the economy, and provides yardstick competition between different areas, together with effective information on local government performance to the central government. Another benefit of Multi-division structure is that the economy can easily withstand macroeconomic shocks. As it is known to us, the Multi-division structure does not exist in Russia. So while this theory can explain why there is so large a gap in economic performance between China and Russia during the transition period, it is not well suited to address whether reforms should be quick or gradual, and cannot permit us to conclude that the piecemeal reform is better than a "big bang" one. As well, the theory fails to explain why China has no institutional infrastructure in place, normally required for economic growth, such as a sound legal system, mature financial markets or a well-defined mechanism to protect and enforce property rights. Despite the lack of all these, China maintains a high growth rate since it adopted the policy of reform and opening.

To understand the difference between gradual reforms and radical ones, and to unravel the apparent paradox of China's economic growth, one needs to delve into the microeconomic mechanism of interactions between formal and informal contracts during transition periods, which is what this chapter seeks to do. Differing from existing literature, the focus here is on contract enforcement or microeconomic governance in the process of economic transition. Due to the existence of asymmetric information (moral hazard and adverse selection), it is necessary for economic contracts to have some kind of governance mechanism. Following Li (2003) here, we also differentiate between two modes of governance: relation-based governance and rule-based governance. The former is self-enforcing in repeated interactions among fixed parties, and thus the information structure for this kind of governance is information of relevant contract variables observable to both parties to the transaction, which do not require verification by a third party (i.e. a court). In short, relation-based governance just requires information observable to both parties, but not verifiable by a third party. In contrast, rule-based governance is an arm's length, impersonal governance mode and the corresponding contracts can be enforced by the third party. So the information structure requires information observable to both parties and verifiable by the third party, which is more demanding.

We will show that the effectiveness of these two modes of governance is limited by the extent of the social division of labor and by the size of the market. The lower the degree of the social division of labor, the more dominant relational contracts will be. With the deepening of the social division of labor and extent of markets, relational contracts will gradually give way to more formal, rules-based contracts. In particular, in an economy with a low level of social division of labor, markets are generally interlinking;[1] that is to say, transactions between the parties will cross multiple markets. In the case of interlinking markets, we prove that the more interlinking the markets are, the larger the set of feasible relational contracts and the more pervasive relational contracts will be in the economy.

The theory has far-reaching implications for the microeconomic governance of the developing economy and transitional economy. In particular, in the economy before transition, the degree of the social division of labor and extent of market is kept low, and the markets are highly interlinking. The interactions between a state-owned organization and its employees span several markets. The organization provides its employees with all kinds of products and services otherwise offered in different specialized markets. So "markets" are highly interlinked to the extent that all the markets are connected or internalized into a highly complicated relational contract. From the perspective of this chapter, changes in governance modes from highly interlinked contracts to less interlinked formal contracts are a microeconomic mechanism behind the economic transition process. The transition from one governance mode to the other involves complex interactions and its success is highly dependent on the types of economic reforms (piecemeal or big-bang) and extent of markets. Radical reforms destroy the viability of self-enforcing contracts, and, under the circumstances of limited division of labor and a small market, may cause governance failure. Gradual reforms allow the enforcement and sustainability of the initial relational contracts to remain until alternative formal contracts take their place, and as a result allow the economy to continue to function well.

This chapter is organized as follows: a benchmark model of the relational contract is provided (single market relational contract), then the benchmark model is generalized to a model of the relational contract within interlinking markets. In the following section previously developed models are used to explain the microeconomic mechanism underpinning the big gap in macroeconomic performance between Chinese-style gradualism and Russian-style radical reforms. In conclusion, there is a further discussion of policy implications for China's current reforms, and future research directions are put forward.

Single-market relational contracts: a benchmark case

Let us first examine a framework of the single market relational contract as a benchmark.[2] Without loss of generality, we consider a bilateral relational contract between a principal and an agent. For simplicity, we assume that they are all risk neutral. By definition, both parties interact infinitely and their common discount factor is $\delta \in (0, 1)$. In each period t, the reserved utility of the principal and the agent is $\bar{V}$ and $\bar{u}$ respectively, representing the highest utility each could respectively gain from alternative opportunities. Each period t could be characterized as a spot contract. The relational contract is composed of an infinite sequence of spot contracts. The agent chooses action $a_t \in A$ at each period. A here denotes the action set of the agent, and a_t denotes the action he chooses at period t, which will yield two possible outputs $y_t \in \{\underline{y}, \bar{y}\}$ at the end of each period. The probability distribution of output y_t is $F(y|a)$, density function $f(x|a)$, satisfying the standard Monotone Likelihood Ratio Property (i.e. $f(y|a)/F(y|a)$

increases with output y_i). Output y is observable to both parties, and unverifiable by a third party; meanwhile a_t is either observable to both parties and unverifiable by the third party, or unobservable to the principal.[3] At the end of each period, after observing the realized output of the agent, the principal will pay the agent W_t, which is composed of one part that is explicitly stated in the contract, w_t, and the other part that is not explicitly written in the contract b_t. This can be described as

$$W_t = w_t + b_t \tag{1}$$

This assumption is widely used. For example, in the labor market, w_t may denote fixed wages in the labor contract, while b_t may denote contingent compensation. Thus, the principal's utility at the end of the period is

$$y_t - W_t \tag{2}$$

and the agent's utility is

$$W_t - \psi(a_t, \theta_t) \tag{3}$$

whereby θ_t denotes the cost parameter only observable to the agent at period t, $\theta_t \in \{\theta_L, \theta_H\}$, $\theta_L \leq \theta_H$. We assume it satisfies independent identical distribution (i.i.d.), and $pr(\theta = \theta_H) = \beta$, $\psi(\cdot)$ denotes the negative utility function of the agent's effort, which satisfies standard assumptions $\psi'(a) > 0$, $\psi''(a) > 0$, $\psi(0, \theta) = 0$, $\psi_\theta \geq 0$, $\psi_{a\theta} > 0$. As we know from (3), this model includes both a moral hazard factor (characterized by endogenous variable a_t) and an adverse selection factor (characterized by exogenous variable θ_t).

The optimization problem for the agent is

$$E_y[y|a] - \psi(a, \theta) \tag{4}$$

where E denotes the expectation operator. For our research problem to be meaningful, we assume under first best action $a^{FB}(\theta)$

$$E_y[y|a^{FB}] - \psi(a^{FB}, \theta) > \bar{s} = \overline{V} + \bar{u} \tag{5}$$

We also assume

$$E_y[y|0] - \psi(0, \theta) \leq \bar{s} \tag{6}$$

(4) together with (5) shows that entering into contract and putting non-negative effort will improve social welfare. The pay-off of the principal and the agent combined is

$$S(a, \theta) \equiv E_y[y|a] - \psi(a, \theta) \tag{7}$$

Formally, a relational contract is the perfect public equilibrium of the infinite game.[4] Players will make the following moves at each period of the game.

(a) The agent decides whether to enter into the contract, and chooses action a_t; (b) The principal decides whether to enter into the contract, and based on realized output chooses payment $b_t(y_i^t)$. The information structure of this game is that during the whole process the agent is able to observe output y_t, his effort a_t, and his cost parameter θ_t. The principal can observe output y_t, while a_t and θ_t are unobservable by the third party. We use an indicator variable to characterize both parties' decisions to enter into the contract. If they all decide to join the contract, $\Lambda = 1$; if at least one party rejects the contract, $\Lambda = 0$. Thus, the standardized expected pay-off of the principal at any time point t is

$$V_t = (1 - \delta) E \sum_{\tau=t}^{\infty} \delta^{t-1} \left[\Lambda(y_t - W_t) + (1 - \Lambda)\overline{V} \right] \tag{8}$$

The normalized expected pay-off of the agent at any time point t is

$$u_t = (1 - \delta) E \sum_{\tau=t}^{\infty} \delta^{t-1} \{ \Lambda [W_\tau - \psi(a_\tau, \theta_\tau)] + (1 - \Lambda)\bar{u} \} \tag{9}$$

The one period case

To better describe the character of relational contract, we first consider a non-relational contract case – a one shot game. In the case of one period, all variables cannot be verified except w, so the principal will not pay the implicit payment b; the agent will choose an action that minimizes his cost; as a result the transaction will never occur. This is an inefficient case, similar to the prisoner's dilemma. We can summarize this intuitive conclusion in Proposition 1.

Proposition 1. *In the case of one period, due to existence of an unenforceable implicit payment b in the contract, players cannot achieve a Pareto improving equilibrium and therefore arrive at an inefficient equilibrium characteristic of the prisoner's dilemma.*

In fact, Proposition 1 can be generalized to any finite period game. Using the backward induction argument, the equilibrium of the last period of the game will be the equilibrium in Proposition 1. Similarly, the equilibrium at the penultimate period all the way up to the equilibrium at the first period will be the equilibrium in Proposition 1. If players rationally expected the equilibrium at period n is like this, they would not have had transaction in the first place. Since it is a finite period game, there is an incentive for both parties to breach the contract. And even if they (or either of them) promise to implement the contract without default, such a promise is not credible because of existence of the unenforceable implicit payment b.

The relational contract

The relational contract comes to improve this inefficient arrangement. If there is a self-enforcing relational contract, that makes the sum of both parties' welfare (surplus) at each period $s > \bar{s}$, compared with inefficient arrangement of a rejected (0) transaction. Both parties can allocate their Pareto improvement part using any linear scheme. In other words, if there is a Pareto improving self-enforcing relational contract, there will be infinite other Pareto improving relational contracts, with the only difference residing in pay-off shares for each player.

A simple example demonstrates this point. If there is a self-enforcing relational contract that makes the overall welfare $s > \bar{s}$ and Pareto improvement is $(s - \bar{s})$, we can always specify a sharing ratio $0 < \lambda < 1$, which leads to the following pay-offs for both parties

$$[\bar{V} + \lambda(s - \bar{s}), \bar{u} + (1 - \lambda)(s - \bar{s})] \tag{10}$$

Obviously, (10) is a Pareto improvement superior to $[\bar{V}, \bar{u}]$. This idea is summarized as the following proposition.

Proposition 2. *If there is a Pareto improving self-enforcing relational contract, there will be infinite Pareto improving relational contracts with the only difference residing in surplus sharing ratios for players.*

We can show this relationship in Figure 2.1. The triangle AOB stands for the no trade area. In this area, there is no room for Pareto improvements. Rectangle $\bar{V}O\bar{u}N$ is the area in which both parties will suffer loss. The area above and to the right of point N will achieve Pareto improvements. We may define Pareto

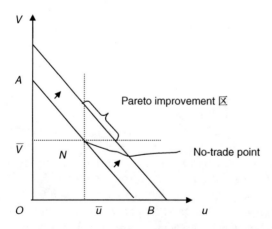

Figure 2.1 Potential Pareto improvements with relational contracts.

improvement as relational rent:

$$RR \equiv s - \bar{s} \tag{11}$$

Since in principle there are infinite Pareto improving self-enforcing relational contracts, what interests us most is the optimal relational contracts. The so-called optimal relational contracts refer to those that maximize overall welfare of both parties. Interestingly, Levin (2003) comes to the conclusion that if there is a relational contract, it can always take the static form. If a relational contract meets the following conditions we call it a static relational contract. On the equilibrium path, the principal always provides the same payment scheme $W_t = w + b(\varphi_t)$, and at each period $a_t = a$. So we have Proposition 3.

Proposition 3. *If optimal relational contracts exist, there must be static optimal contracts.*

Proposition 3 tells us that since both parties are risk neutral it is equivalent for the agent to receive current direct compensation and to gain compensation from subsequent equilibrium. So it is always possible to smooth out transfers between them and their actions across periods. As a result a static contract with the same actions and pay-offs always exists.

The above analysis suggests that it is enough for us to focus on static optimal contracts, though there may be many relational contracts. Let us now consider what is the optimal static contract is. We use u^* and $(s^* - u^*)$ to denote the agent's and the principal's pay-off under optimal static contract respectively. a^* is the agent's effort. The optimal cooperative surplus is

$$s^* \equiv \max_{a} \ (1-\delta)E\left[v - \psi(a,\theta)|a\right] + \delta E\left[s^*|a^*\right] \tag{12}$$

$$\text{s.t. } a^* \in \arg\max \left\{E\left[w + b(\varphi_t) + \frac{\delta}{1-\delta}u^*|a\right] - \psi(a,\theta)\right\} \text{ (IC)} \tag{13}$$

$$b(\varphi_t) + \frac{\delta}{1-\delta}u^* \geq \frac{\delta}{1-\delta}\bar{u} \qquad \text{(PC-A)} \tag{14}$$

$$-b(\varphi_t) + \frac{\delta}{1-\delta}(s^* - u^*) \geq \frac{\delta}{1-\delta}\bar{V} \qquad \text{(PC-B)} \tag{15}$$

where (13) is the agent's incentive compatible constraint, which ensures that the agent has enough incentive to choose a^* (as it brings him the highest pay-off); (14) is the agent's participation constraint, which implies that once the agent exits, he will leave the contract forever. This assumption tallies with what we observe in the real world. If a relational contract comes to an end, it will never function again. The threat of exit forever is actually the most serious threat the agent imposes on the principal, which guarantees the most self-enforcing relational contracts. (15) is the principal's participation constraint.

We can rewrite (14) as

$$\frac{\delta}{1-\delta}(u^* - \bar{u}) \geq -b(\varphi_t) \tag{16}$$

The expression on the right part of (16) is the agent's incentive to breach the contract, the maximum value of which is $-\underset{\varphi}{\inf}\, b(\varphi)$. It shows that, to sustain the self-enforcing contract, the discounted value of the agent's loss resulting from breaching the contract must exceed his incentive to breach the contract. Similarly, (15) can be rewritten as

$$\frac{\delta}{1-\delta}[(s^* - u^*) - \overline{V}] \geq b(\varphi_t) \tag{17}$$

We may rewrite it as

$$\frac{\delta}{1-\delta}[V^* - \overline{V}] \geq b(\varphi_t) \tag{18}$$

The expression on the right of (18) is actually the principal's incentive to breach the contract, the maximum value of which is $\underset{\varphi}{\sup}\, b(\varphi)$. So (18) tells us that to sustain the self-enforcing contract, from the perspective of the principal, the principal's future loss resulting from breaching the contract must exceed his current incentive to breach the contract.

Combining (17) and (18), we obtain

$$\frac{\delta}{1-\delta}(s^* - \bar{s}) \geq \left(\underset{\varphi}{\sup}\, b(\varphi) - \underset{\varphi}{\inf}\, b(\varphi) \right) \quad \text{(SEC)} \tag{19}$$

We call (19) the self-enforcing constraint. Any contract that satisfies (12) and (19) is self-enforcing and static optimal.[5]

Interlinking markets and relational contracts

Previously relational contracts were examined in the case of a single market. The most important character of a transition economy or a developing economy is that the degree of the social division of labor in the economy is low and there are no highly specialized markets. In countries with a more advanced social division of labor, people interact with others in various specialized markets. In contrast, in developing countries with low social division of labor, the transactions between two people go across several markets. We call this phenomenon "interlinking markets". A typical example is agricultural markets in developing countries. Tenants and landlords interact on produce markets (landlords may buy food from tenants), on labor markets (landlords buy tenants' labor), on credit markets (landlords may provide loans to tenants), and on insurance markets (landlords provide some form of insurance to tenants, e.g. through sharecropping). In planned and transition economies, the relationships between organizations and their employees also have the some of the properties of "interlinking markets". Organizations and their employees interact across multiple markets including product, labor, insurance, and financial markets. In this sense, changing into a market economy is a transition from interlinking markets to specialized markets. So characterizing the influence of interlinking markets on people's behavior concerning contracts is an important dimension in the study of economic development and transition.

This section considers interlinking markets in the framework of relational contracts. First we discuss the effects of interlinking markets on relational contract equilibrium. Then we examine the influence of the social division of labor on organizational forms. Theoretically this section is a step forward from the current relational contract theories that focus on interactions between the principal and the agent in a single market. The limitations of these theories are obvious in terms of their failure to consider developing or transition economies with low social division of labor. As well, interlinking markets are generally present even in developed countries.

To better compare and contrast the equilibrium of interlinking market relational contracts with the one of single market relational contracts, unless otherwise stated, we will continue to use the structure and parameters in previous models above. We assume relational contracts in interlinking markets are between the same pair of the principal and the agent interacting on different markets. For simplicity, we consider two markets without loss of generality.

Relational contracts in two interlinking markets

Let us consider two spot contracts to identify differences in two different markets. The interlinking market will be characterized by interactions between the principal and the agent across the two markets. $\overline{V}_1$ and $\bar{u}_1$ are used to denote their respective reserved utility for interaction in the first market at each period (i.e. the highest pay-off of outside opportunities). $\overline{V}_2$ and $\bar{u}_2$ are used to denote their respective reserved utility for interaction in the second market at each period.

The agent chooses action $a_{1t} \in A_1$ in the first market at each period, and the action yields two possible outputs $\tilde{y}_{1t} \in \{y_1, \bar{y}_1\}$ at the end of each period. The probability distribution is $F_1(y_{1t}|a_{1t})$, and the density function is $f_1(y_{1t}|a_{1t})$, which we assume satisfies the standard Monotone Likelihood Ratio Property. Similarly, the agent chooses action $a_{2t} \in A_2$ in the second market, and yielding two possible outputs $\tilde{y}_{2t} \in [y_2, \bar{y}_2]$ at the end of each period. Outputs in the above markets are observable to both parties and unverifiable by a third party. For simplicity, the agent's action is either observable to both parties and unverifiable by the third party, or unobservable to the principal (in the case of moral hazard).

At the end of each period t, after observing the realized output of the agent, the principal will pay the agent W_{1t} in the first market, which is composed of two parts:

$$W_{1t} = w_{1t} + b_{1t} \tag{20}$$

where w_{1t} and b_{1t} denote explicit part and implicit part respectively. Thus, the principal's utility at the end of the period t is

$$y_{1t} - W_{1t} \tag{21}$$

The agent's utility is

$$W_{1t} - \psi_1(a_{1t}, \theta_{1t}) \tag{22}$$

where θ_{1t} denotes cost parameter only observable to the agent at period t, $\theta_{1t} \in \{\theta_{1L}, \theta_{1H}\}$, and $\theta_{1L} < \theta_{1H}$. We assume it satisfies independent identical distribution (i.i.d), and $pr(\theta_1 = \theta_{1H}) = \beta_1$. $\psi(\cdot)$ denotes the negative utility function of the agent's effort in the first market, which satisfies standard assumptions $\psi_1'(a_1) > 0 \psi_1''(a_1) > 0$, $\psi_1(0, \theta) = 0$, $\psi_{1\theta_1} \geq 0$, and $\psi_{1a_1\theta_1} > 0$.

Similarly, we can describe behaviors of two parties in the second market with a minor change of subscript 1 into 2. After characterizing the contractual context of the principal and agent in interlinking markets, we can now investigate the interactions between two markets.

The fact that static contracts exist tells us that actually it is enough for the principal and the agent to maximize pay-off at the current period. If at least one party cheats (for example, the principal does not make payment b, or the agent shirks his duty) they will come back to an inefficient no-transaction equilibrium. We assume under the first best action $a^{FB}(\theta)$

$$E_{y_{1t}}\left[y_{1t}|a_1^{FB}\right] + E_{y_{2t}}\left[y_{2t}|a_2^{FB}\right] - \psi_1\left(a_1^{FB}, \theta_1\right) - \psi_2\left(a_2^{FB}, \theta_2\right) > \overline{S}_1 + \overline{S}_2 \tag{23}$$

where $\overline{S}_1 = \overline{V}_1 + \bar{u}_1$, $\overline{S}_2 = \overline{V}_2 + \bar{u}_2$. In addition, we assume

$$E_{y_{1t}}[y_{1t}|0] + E_{y_{2t}}[y_{2t}|0] - \psi_1(0, \theta_1) - \psi_2(0, \theta_2) \leq \overline{S}_1 + \overline{S}_2 \tag{24}$$

The cooperative surplus of the principal and the agent is

$$S_{Int}(a_1, a_2, \theta_1, \theta_2) = E_{y_1}[y_1|a_1] + E_{y_2}[y_2|a_2] - \psi_1(a_1) - \psi_2(a_2) \tag{25}$$

We assume that if one party breaches the contract, the other will exit forever, so they come back to a no-trade situation. Using index variable $\tilde{\Lambda}$ to characterize both parties' decisions to enter into the interlinking market relational contract, if they all decide to join the contract, $\tilde{\Lambda} = 1$; if at least one party rejects the contract, $\tilde{\Lambda} = 0$. Thus, the normalized expected pay-off of the principal at any time point t is

$$V_t^{int} = (1-\delta)E\sum_{\tau=t}^{\infty}\delta^{t-1}\left[\tilde{\Lambda}(y_{1t}-W_{1t})+\tilde{\Lambda}(y_{2t}-W_{2t})+(1-\tilde{\Lambda})(\overline{V}_1+\overline{V}_2)\right]$$

$$(26)$$

The standardized expected pay-off of the agent at any time point t is

$$u_t^{int} = (1-\delta)E\sum_{\tau=t}^{\infty}\delta^{t-1}\left[\tilde{\Lambda}(W_{1t}-\psi_{1t}(a_{1\tau},\theta_{1\tau}))+\tilde{\Lambda}(W_{2t}-\psi_{2t}(a_{2\tau},\theta_{2\tau}))\right.$$

$$\left.-(1-\tilde{\Lambda})(\bar{u}_1+\bar{u}_2)\right] \qquad (27)$$

To compare with the case of a single market, we first consider one period case (the non-relational contract).

The one period case

In the case of one period, even in interlinking markets, all variables cannot be verified except w, so the principal will not pay contingent implicit payment b in one time interaction. Thus non-relational contracts at the first period or during any finite periods cannot last. To keep consistency and symmetry, we summarize this simple conclusion in the following proposition.

Proposition 4. *Implicit contracts cannot be achieved in one-time transaction on the interlinking markets.*

The relational contract

In interlinking markets, if there is a self-enforcing relational contract, that makes the sum of both parties' surplus at each period $S_1+S_2 > \overline{S}_1+\overline{S}_2$, compared with inefficient arrangement of no trade. As in the case of the single market, both parties can allocate their Pareto improvement part through any linear scheme, providing infinite Pareto improving relational contracts.

As in the case of single market, if we specify a sharing ratio of $0 < \lambda < 1$ to allocate Pareto improvement $(S_1+S_2)-(\overline{S}_1+\overline{S}_2)$, we achieve the following pay-offs for two parties:

$$\left(\overline{V}_1+\overline{V}_2+\lambda\left[(S_1+S_2)-(\overline{S}_1+\overline{S}_2)\right],\bar{u}_1+\bar{u}_2+(1-\lambda)\left[(S_1+S_2)-(\overline{S}_1+\overline{S}_2)\right]\right)$$

Obviously the above expression is a Pareto improvement on $[\overline{V}_1+\overline{V}_2,\bar{u}_1+\bar{u}_2]$. We can summarize this in the following proposition.

Proposition 5. *In interlinking markets if there is a Pareto improving self-enforcing relational contract, there will be infinite Pareto improvement relational* contracts, with the only difference residing in the surplus sharing ratios for the parties.

Now we can relax our assumptions on the relationships between V and $\overline{V}$, u and $\bar{u}$ and S and $\overline{S}$ by assuming that the outside opportunity cost is variable (for example, a new opportunity appears because of a change in market environment). To start a comparative static analysis of outside opportunity cost, we consider some possible combinations of Pareto improvement.

Case 1. $u_1 > \bar{u}_1, V_1 > \overline{V}_1, u_2 > \bar{u}_2, V_2 > \overline{V}_2$

In this case there are Pareto improvements in each market. This case has no qualitative difference from relational contracts on a single market. The only difference is that both parties' surpluses are higher. So no further discussion on this case.

Case 2. $u_1 < \bar{u}_1, V_1 > \overline{V}_1, u_2 > \bar{u}_2, V_2 > \overline{V}_2, u_1 + u_2 > \bar{u}_1 + \bar{u}_2, S_1 + S_2 > \overline{S}_1 + \overline{S}_2$

This case implies that although the agent has a tempting outside opportunity to deviate in the first market ($u_1 < \bar{u}_1$), it is an improvement for him to join the interlinking relational contracts (we assume here that he joins the relational contracts on either both markets or neither) since he gains enough compensation from the relational contract in the second market ($u_1 + u_2 > \bar{u}_1 + \bar{u}_2$).

Case 3. $u_1 > \bar{u}_1, V_1 < \overline{V}_1, u_2 > \bar{u}_2, V_2 > \overline{V}_2, V_1 + V_2 > \overline{V}_1 + \overline{V}_2, S_1 + S_2 > \overline{S}_1 + \overline{S}_2$

This case demonstrates that although the principal has a tempting outside opportunity to deviate in the first market ($V_1 < \overline{V}_1$), it is an improvement for him to join the interlinking relational contracts since he gains enough compensation from the relational contract in the second market ($V_1 + V_2 > \overline{V}_1 + \overline{V}_2$).

Case 4. $u_1 > \bar{u}_1, V_1 > \overline{V}_1, u_2 < \bar{u}_2, V_2 > \overline{V}_2, u_1 + u_2 > \bar{u}_1 + \bar{u}_2, S_1 + S_2 > \overline{S}_1 + \overline{S}_2$

Similarly, this case demonstrates that although the agent has a tempting outside opportunity to deviate in the second market ($u_2 < \bar{u}_2$), it is an improvement for him to join the interlinking relational contracts since he gains enough compensation from the relational contract in the first market ($u_1 + u_2 > \bar{u}_1 + \bar{u}_2$).

Case 5. $u_1 > \bar{u}_1, V_1 > \overline{V}_1, u_2 > \bar{u}_2, V_2 < \overline{V}_2, V_1 + V_2 > \overline{V}_1 + \overline{V}_2, S_1 + S_2 > \overline{S}_1 + \overline{S}_2$

This case demonstrates that although the principal has a tempting outside opportunity to deviate in the second market ($V_2 < \overline{V}_2$), it is an improvement for him to enter into both interlinking relational contracts since he gains enough compensation from the relational contract in the first market.

Case 6. $u_1 < \bar{u}_1, V_1 < \overline{V}_1, u_2 > \bar{u}_2, V_2 > \overline{V}_2, V_1 + V_2 > \overline{V}_1 + \overline{V}_2, u_1 + u_2 > \bar{u}_1 + \bar{u}_2, S_1 + S_2 > \overline{S}_1 + \overline{S}_2$

In Case 6, although there is tempting opportunity in the relational contract in the first market for both the principal and the agent, it is a welfare improvement for them to enter into the interlinking relational contract because they are compensated in the second market. It seems a little perplexing. One may ask why they join the contract in the first place if the relational contract in the first market does them no good. While we list this case for the sake of completeness, in the real world this may be a case in which players both enter the markets for technological reasons.

Case 7. $u_1 > \bar{u}_1, V_1 > \overline{V}_1, u_2 < \bar{u}_2, V_2 < \overline{V}_2, V_1 + V_2 > \overline{V}_1 + \overline{V}_2, u_1 + u_2 > \bar{u}_1 + \bar{u}_2,$
$S_1 + S_2 > \overline{S}_1 + \overline{S}_2$

As opposed to Case 6, Case 7 shows that although there is tempting opportunity in the relational contract in the second market for both the principal and the agent to deviate, their welfare improves if they join the interlinking relational contract because they receive benefits in the first market.

Certainly there are other possible combinations, but we have just focused on certain interesting cases. We find from these cases that we can greatly expand the set of viable relational contracts by introducing interlinking markets, which means transactions are possible that would otherwise be unfeasible in single markets. We can summarize this in the following proposition.

Proposition 6. *Market interlinking greatly expands the feasible relational contract set, by making inefficient single market transactions possible under and through interlinked relational contracts.*

This proposition has strong implications for the transition economy with less developed social division of labor. In these economies, due to low social division of labor, specialized markets (interactions between different people on different markets) are less developed and a large amount of transaction takes place among the same group of people in interlinking markets. A natural implication derived from Proposition 6 is that in an economy with low social division of labor, a large amount of transaction takes place in interlinking markets. That is to say, the same parties interact on different markets. The more advanced the social division of labor, the more weakly markets are interlinked, and the relational contract is of less significance.

In light of Proposition 3, we can demonstrate the following proposition.

Proposition 7. *If optimal relational contracts exist, there must be static optimal contracts.*

Since both parties are risk neutral, it is equivalent for them to receive current direct compensation and to gain compensation from subsequent equilibrium. So it is always possible to smooth out their pay-offs across periods. In theory, under interlinking markets, their pay-offs are "bundled" on both markets in each period. Thus their utility possibility frontier will differ from that in the single market. In particular, in Case 1 their utility possibility frontiers will move outward.

Further considering Case 1, we know from the above structure that although in theory there is an infinite number of relational contracts, we can just focus on the optimal static relational contracts without loss of generality. Let u_1^* and u_2^* be the agent's pay-offs on the first and the second market respectively under the optimal static contract. $(S_1^* - u_1^*)$ and $(S_2^* - u_2^*)$ denote the principal's pay-offs on the first and the second market respectively. a_1^* and a_2^* are the agent's optimal effort. The optimal cooperative surplus is

$$S^* \equiv \max_{a_1, a_2} (1-\delta) E[y_1 + y_2 - \psi_1(a_1, \theta_1)|a_1 - \psi_2(a_2, \theta_2)|a_2]$$

$$+ \delta E[S^*|a_1^*, a_2^*] \qquad (28)$$

$$\text{s.t. } a_1^*, a_2^* \in \arg\max \left\{ E\left[w_1 + b_1(y_1) + \frac{\delta}{1-\delta} u_1^*|a_1 - \psi_1(a_1, \theta_1) \right] - \psi_1(a_1, \theta_1) \right.$$

$$\left. + E\left[w_2 + b_2(y_2) + \frac{\delta}{1-\delta} u_2^*|a_2 \right] - \psi_2(a_2, \theta_2) \right\} \quad (\text{IC}) \qquad (29)$$

$$b_1(y_1) + b_2(y_2) + \frac{\delta}{1-\delta}(u_1^* + u_2^*) \geq \frac{\delta}{1-\delta}(\bar{u}_1 + \bar{u}_2) \quad (\text{PC-A}) \qquad (30)$$

$$-b_1(y_1) - b_2(y_2) + \frac{\delta}{1-\delta}(S_1^* + S_2^* - u_1^* - u_2^*) \geq \frac{\delta}{1-\delta}(\overline{V}_1 + \overline{V}_2) \quad (\text{PC-B})$$

$$(31)$$

where variables with the sign * are the optimal values. (29) is the agent's incentive compatible constraint, which means it will bring him the maximum pay-off if he joins the contract and chooses the first best action. (30) is the agent's participation constraint, which implies that once the agent exits, he will leave the contract forever. The threat of exiting forever is actually the most serious threat the agent imposes on the principal, which allows self-enforcing relational contracts. (31) is the principal's participation constraint. We can rewrite (30) as

$$\frac{\delta}{1-\delta}((u_1^* + u_2^*) - (\bar{u}_1 + \bar{u}_2)) \geq -(b_1(y_1) + b_2(y_2)) \qquad (32)$$

The expression on the right of (32) is the agent's incentive to breach the contract, the maximum value of which is $-(\inf b_1(y_1) + \inf b_2(y_2))$. To attract the agent to join the interlinking market relational contract, (32) may be rewritten as

$$\frac{\delta}{1-\delta}((u_1^* + u_2^*) - (\bar{u}_1 + \bar{u}_2)) \geq -(\inf b_1(y_1) + \inf b_2(y_2)) \qquad (33)$$

Similarly, (31) may take the following form:

$$\frac{\delta}{1-\delta}(S_1^* + S_2^* - u_1^* - u_2^* - \overline{V}_1 - \overline{V}_2) \geq b_1(y_1) + b_2(y_2) \qquad (34)$$

The expression on the right of (34) is actually the principal's incentive to breach the contract, the maximum value of which is $(\sup b_1(y_1) + \sup b_2(y_2))$. So, to attract the principal to enter into the relational contract, we may rewrite (34) as

$$\frac{\delta}{1-\delta}(S_1^* + S_2^* - u_1^* - u_2^* - \overline{V}_1 - \overline{V}_2) \geq \sup b_1(y_1) + \sup b_2(y_2) \qquad (35)$$

Combining (33) and (35), we obtain

$$\frac{\delta}{1-\delta}(S_1^* + S_2^* - \overline{S}_1 - \overline{S}_2) \geq \sup b_1(y_1) + \sup b_2(y_2) - \inf b_1(y_1)$$

$$- \inf b_2(y_2) \quad \text{(SEC)} \tag{36}$$

(36) is a self-enforcing constraint or dynamic enforcing constraint. According to our construct, any contract that satisfies (29) and (36) is self-enforcing and static optimal in interlinking markets.

We have completed the characterization of the interlinking market relational contract. Now we will compare and contrast relational contracts in interlinking markets and on a single market. First, we notice that in Case 1, that is, $u_1 > \bar{u}_1$, $V_1 > \overline{V}_1$, $u_2 > \bar{u}_2$, $V_2 > \overline{V}_2$, there will be more rent from relational contracts in interlinking markets than from those on a single market. In other words, the rents from two single markets are bundled. The surplus cannot be realized with one shot or finite interactions. Increasing δ will increase the target function and relax the incentive constraints and self-enforcing constraints, making relational contract more feasible. Second, in other cases, a separately inefficient transaction and efficient transaction are bundled with a relational contract.

The interactions between market interlinkage and relational contracts may be a key to understanding the relationship between the degree of the social division of labor and economic organization. To some extent, we can say that the lower the degree of the social division of labor, the higher the market interlinkage, the more feasible the relational contract, while its welfare implications are ambiguous.

There may be another mechanism through which division of labor affects the sustainability of relational contract. For example, Kranton (1996) shows that reciprocal transactions and arm's length market transactions are both self-sustaining equilibrium. With more people participating in reciprocal trade, the arm's length market will become very thin and hence the search cost will be high. In this case, reciprocal trade is sustainable despite its inefficiency and vice versa. In terms of our theory, the thinness of market and associated search costs can be reduced to $\bar{u}$ and $\overline{V}$. In the case of a thin arm's length market, $\bar{u}$ and $\overline{V}$ are low, rendering relational contracts more sustainable; otherwise, $\bar{u}$ and $\overline{V}$ will be high, tightening the incentive compatible constraints (28), and participation constraints (29) and (30), in the optimal relational contract. We can summarize this point in Proposition 8.

Proposition 8. *The degree of the social division of labor will influence the thickness of the arm's length market and the search cost. The thinner the market is, the higher the search cost. So the outside opportunity cost of the relational contract $\bar{u}$ and $\overline{V}$ will be low, making relational contracts easier to sustain. If the arm's length market is thick, the search cost will be low, and the outside opportunity cost of the relational contract $\bar{u}$ and $\overline{V}$ will be high. If $\bar{u}$ and $\overline{V}$ are high enough to exceed the critical points $\hat{u}$ and $\hat{V}$, then a relational contract will not be sustainable.*

We have examined interactions between relational contracts on two markets. The analysis can be easily generalized to $n(n > 2)$ markets, and the qualitative conclusions drawn under the two markets still hold, so we will not give a detailed analysis. One point we would like to emphasize from the Pareto improving combinations analyzed under two interlinking markets is that the greater the number of interlinking markets, the more viable relational contracts will exist. We can summarize this conclusion in the following proposition.

Proposition 9. *The more interlinking markets (larger n) there are, the more feasible relational contracts there will be, rendering otherwise unfeasible relational contracts ($\tilde{n}(\tilde{n} < n)$) possible in an interlinked market.*

Relational contracts and the underlying mechanism of economic transition: China versus Russia

We can now analyze the difference in microeconomic governance of the transition economy between China and Russia using the theory developed above. Prior to recent reforms China and Russia were both planned economies. In such economies, the relationship between an organization and its members is in essence a relational contract. People may spend their entire lives working in one place, for one organization. Such a long-term game makes relational contracts technically possible. In addition, in classic planned economies the extent of the market is very limited, which makes the opportunity cost of relational contracts very low. Combining these two points, we find that relational contracts are sustainable. In reality, the organizations in a planned economy interact with their members covering several "markets", creating multiple opportunities for relational contracts.

In planned economies, the interlinked relational contract is highly sustainable and self-enforcing. "Shock therapy" destroys self-sustaining relational contracts almost overnight before governance based on formal contracts is in place. According to our model, governance by formal contracts is dependent on the degree of social division of labor and the extent of markets, both of which are and will be limited for a long time in transition economies. Thus relational contracts will be dominant modes of governance for a long time to come. As compared to Russia, China took a totally different way of reform. Quite contrary to Russia, China's gradualism keeps relational contracts sustainable during the transition. In terms of governance structure, transition is nothing but the same process with more formal contracts replacing relational ones.

The nature and role of some unique institutional arrangements in China's transition can be reconsidered in light of the theory. Among all the institutions, TVEs (township and village enterprises) made the most important contribution in the first 15 years of the transition. In their heyday in the early 1990s TVEs accounted for 27 percent of industrial output and nearly two-thirds of the non-state sector in industrial output, while the private sector accounted for only 15 percent of industrial output. TVEs are neither private firms nor public firms.

Even though managers of TVEs have considerable autonomy in their day-to-day operations, community governments play an active role in investment and finance decisions, management selection and in allocating after-tax profits for public expenditures. For a long time this has posed a puzzle for economists since it is usually assumed that governmental control will lead to inefficiency.

Our theory can shed some light on the phenomenon.[6] In the early years of China's transition, especially in the rural areas, the markets (labor, credit, product, land, etc.) were either missing or imperfect. In this case, interlinked contracts (explicit or implicit) can achieve Pareto improving allocations by creating contracts that otherwise would not exist. Governments and entrepreneurs interact over several markets. Governments provide entrepreneurs with credit and land, and also help them to market their products. They provide legal and political protections. When the market develops and becomes more specialized, the advantages of interlinked contracts should decline, and the interlinkages should unravel along the way. This appears to be the case after the mid-1990s, when specialized markets were more mature, and most TVEs were restructured into private firms.

The restructure of state-owned enterprises (SOEs) constitutes another case in point. Unlike the radical approach to restructuring of SOEs, in the early stages of restructuring Chinese SOEs, the government continued for some time to provide employees with housing, medical care and other welfare programs, as before. This institutional arrangement can also be considered as an interlinking contract. When housing, medical care and other markets are missing or imperfect, this arrangement achieves an efficient allocation and reduces the social cost of the transition. In particular, the in-house provision of certain services (such as a kindergarten) remained during the restructuring of the SOEs for a long time until they were spun off or "socialized" (*she hui hua*).

Putting these examples together, we can see that the emergence of TVEs to a large extent relaxed the constraints facing the reform of SOEs, by absorbing the excess labor and other resources released from the SOEs. To make the restructuring of SOEs even smoother, the government kept injecting money from banks to the SOEs for extended periods after the reform was initiated. At the first sight, the weak banking system appears to be a burden for the reform; however, it actually helped soften the negative effects of the restructuring of other sectors, including SOEs.

This leads us to ask, who has financed China's recent growth? Again, our theory can shed some light on the question. The answer lies in informal finance, or relational finance, which occurs between members in a community. A general feature of relational finance is that the credit transaction is also implicitly or explicitly interlinked with other transactions. This interlinked contract can not only permit Pareto improving allocations when the markets (especially the credit market) are imperfect, but may also act as an effective enforcement mechanism when there is limited enforcement, especially in rural areas. Hence, different interest rates of relational credit differ from place to place in China as they reflect differing interlinking contexts.

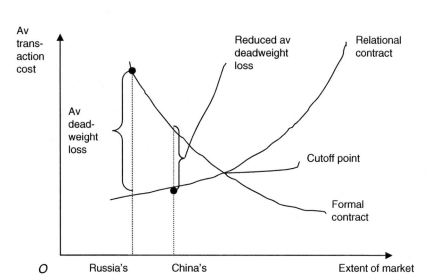

Figure 2.2 The dynamics of relational contracts and formal contracts.

The above are some cases of interlinked contracts in China's economic transition, which provide the needed social capital that constitutes an effective substitute for formal enforcement mechanisms, a general lack of which characterizes the Chinese transition economy. In contrast, Russia took a quite different approach to transition. The quick liberalization and privatization made the original relational contract unsustainable, and the mafia arose as an alternative.[7]

Hence, we can explain the Chinese paradox introduced at the start of this chapter. China achieved its miraculous economic development, despite a general lack of formal and legal institutions, because relational contracts are self-enforcing and legal or institutional enforcement is not necessary. Figure 2.2 shows a schematic comparison between the governance dynamics of China and Russia during transition.[8]

Concluding remarks

Within the framework of interlinked relational contracts, we can characterize the interaction between development and institutions and shed some light on the nature and dynamics of the gradual and radical approaches to economic transition. The main idea of this chapter can be summarized as follows: efficient governance structure (contractual form) is limited by the extent of the market. The less the extent of the market, the more important relational contracts is and vice versa.

Nevertheless, the transition from relation-based governance to rule-based governance is not necessarily smooth, with the increased extent of the market.

The East Asian crises in the late 1990s show this point. At the threshold point of the two governances, there may be a void of governance, leading to disruption and destruction to the economy. In this sense, the real challenge for China's transition is when and how to introduce a system of formal institutions well before the threshold is reached. Order without law may not be sustainable with further development.

From the perspective of contract theory, this chapter constitutes a starting point towards a more fully developed theory of interlinked relational contracts. We have only considered the viability of such contracts. A future avenue would be to explore the equilibrium in the case of moral hazard, adverse selection with interlinked relational contracts, and to see how the conclusions in the standard contract theory carry over in these cases.

3 Markets, contracts and economic growth

Market expansion, with the deepening of the division of labor, is one of the most important sources of economic growth. Institutionally, transformation from relationship-based governance to rule-based governance is the great transformation during the process of modern economic growth. Can this process be characterized by a simple theoretical framework? Economists as early as Adam Smith argued that the expansion of the market size can deepen the division of labor and economic growth, but it leaves such questions open as the micro mechanism that accounts for why development of mankind and economic growth must be dependent on expansion of market size and the relationship between the governance and market size. What will unfold in this chapter is the interaction between economic growth and market expansion: given the market size, economic growth will be accompanied by a diminishing marginal return of capital (or diminishing marginal utility of goods), while with market expansion, marginal return of capital (or marginal utility of goods) can be increased by using complementary factors (or goods) on other markets, thereby further driving economic growth. *Ex ante* market expansion decisions may face the risks associated with increasing transaction costs. The larger the market size and the more people are involved in the transaction, the higher the *ex post* probability of loss-making for market expansion. Rule-based contracts are thus needed to compensate relevant losses. Our story provides insights for understanding the economic opening and globalization process, world economy development history and modern China economic development, as well as the relationship between contractual forms and economic development.

Economic growth is a historic process driven by factor accumulation, technological progress and institutional changes. Given technological level and institutional structure, economic growth will be fuelled by factor accumulation, but factor accumulation will ultimately lead to diminishing marginal return. Therefore, from a historical perspective, economic growth is mainly spurred by technological progress and institutional change. The existing literature generally deals with the two growth drivers separately: the growth theories of the Solow model (Solow 1956) investigate exogenous or endogenous technological progress, while the new institutional school represented by North examines the underpinning institutions (especially property right institutions) of economic growth. North and Wallis (1994) constitute an exception. They look at institutional change and technological progress from an organizational perspective, which is a step forward from Coase and Williamson. According to the Coase theorem (Coase 1937), the existence of the firm is to save market transaction costs and the boundary of a firm in equilibrium is determined by the point at which the marginal transaction cost in the organization is equal to the marginal transaction cost of the market. Later, the work of Williamson (1975, 1985) focuses on what kinds of transaction cost (e.g. asset specificity, frequency of transition) determine the choice between the firm and the market. All his work identified optimal institutional choice or contractual forms to minimize transaction costs given the technology level. According to this theory, institutional evolution will lead to decreasing transaction costs in the process of economic development. However, the empirical research of North and Wallis (1986) shows that during the century 1870–1970, the percentage of transaction costs in GDP in the US rose from 25 to 45 percent. They argue that economic organizations simultaneously choose technology and institutions to minimize total cost – the sum of transformation costs related to technological choice and transaction costs related to institutional choice. That is to say, there is substitution and/or complementary relationship between technological choice and institutional choice. However, they simply introduced a new variable into the production function of the firm and hence the interaction between technological choice and institutional choice is still a "black box" in their theoretical framework. Moreover, their theory is static and thus cannot account for changes in technological choice and institutional choice over time.

One of the main purposes that theories serve is to explain historical and real world stylized facts. The theory presented in this chapter not only accounts for the fact observed by North that the service sector plays a greater role in a more developed economy, but also offers a perspective from which the following three important facts in economic development can be explained.

The first fact is that, historically, economic growth itself is not a modern phe-nomenon. According to Maddison (2001), in the Annals of the first millennium AD, there was virtually no increase in the per capita GDP, so economic growth simply did not exist. Even during the period of 820 years from 1000 to 1820, economic growth was very slow; the world average growth rate of per capita GDP was only around 50 percent. After 1820, world economic growth sped up, with per capita GDP increasing by eight times so far. Overall, a trend of accelerating economic growth is obvious (see Figure 3.1).

The second fact is that the economic growth path varies from country to country. In particular, in the first millennium, Asia played a decisive role in the world economy. For instance in 1000 AD, Asia (excluding Japan) accounted for more than two-thirds of the world's GDP, compared with less than 9 percent for Western Europe. But by 1820, Asia's position had weakened relative to Western Europe, with the former accounting for 56 percent of the world's GDP and the latter 24 percent. Specifically, there was sharp contrast between the development of China and Western Europe. In technological and economic development,

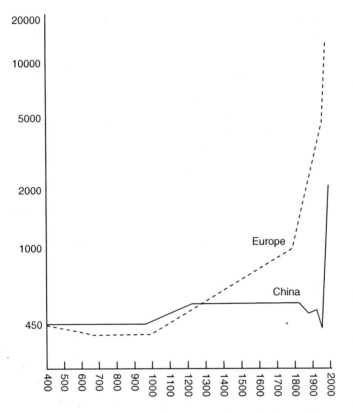

Figure 3.1 Changes in per capita GDP in China and Western Europe, 400–1998 AD.
Note: Log for vertical axis measures.
Source: Maddison (2001).

China had been ahead of Western Europe over a long time, and even calculated on the basis of GDP per capita, Western Europe did not surpass China until around 1300 (see Figure 3.1). In terms of total GDP, China remained the world's largest economy till 1820, taking up 34.2 percent of the world's GDP (Maddison 1998). However, the technological revolution and industrial revolution in the modern sense occurred in Western Europe, and so did institutional innovations and organizational innovations in the socioeconomic and political areas. The "Great Divergence" (Pomeranz 2000) is a recurrent theme that fascinates social scientists, noted by Dr Joseph Needham in his discourse on the history of Chinese technologies.

   The third fact is that the expansion of market extent, technology and innovation system, place the scope of economies far beyond the boundaries of nation-state. Globalization has become an important trend in human development. As is the case with the European Union, where national boundaries blur, other parts of the world (e.g. North America) show a similar trend. This shows that technological change may be one of the internal factors that determine actual country borders.

This chapter provides a simple theory to understand the above phenomena related to the process of economic development and modernization. To this end, the individual decisions on trade expansion, and the factor complementariness brought about by the market expansion are explored. The dynamics of market size, economic growth and contractual forms over time are discussed. This chapter can be regarded as a growth theory except that the focus is the agent's decision on market size rather than the trade-off between consumption and capital accumulation as highlighted by standard growth theories. This departure from the standard theories of economic growth constitutes a contribution of this chapter to the growth theory literature.

This is also different from the new classical economics developed by Yang and Ng (1993). They consider the trade-off between technological advances and transaction costs brought about by deepening division of labor rather than the interaction between economic growth and market expansion. What are more relevant to our theme are studies by Li (2003) and Dixit (2003). Li distinguishes between relation-based governance structure and rule-based governance structure and shows that an effective governance structure depends on the size of the market: when the market is relatively small, relational governance is more effective; and when the market is large and beyond a certain extent, rule-based governance would be more effective. The idea is that relational governance involves relatively low fixed transaction costs, but higher marginal transaction costs, and the contrary is true for rule-based governance. He also uses this framework to explain the successes and failures of the East Asian model. Despite the insights, Li lacks formal models and the mechanisms are not clear. In particular, economic agents' market expansion decisions and the structure of transaction costs remains a black box in his paper, and economic growth is not incorporated into his theory as an endogenous variable.

Dixit (2003) formalized Li's ideas to a large degree. In particular, he develops a circular matching model and shows the scope of honest transaction beyond which deceit will arise to make the transaction unprofitable. But since his focus is on the conflict between the scope of transaction and deceit, he does not characterize the relationship between market size and division of labor, and there was no account for economic growth. Wang (2005, 2006) extends the relational contract in a single market to that with interlinking markets and explores the intrinsic relation between the degree of social division of labor and the contractual forms: the lower the degree of division of labor, the stronger the interlinkage between markets (i.e. transactions between the agents are across several markets) and the more important relational contracts will be; the higher the degree of division of labor, the more important the formal contract (implemented by a third party like a court) will be. Although he established the relationship between the degree of division of labor and the contractual form, he also left the relation to economic growth unaccounted for. North, Wallis and Weingast (2006) relate social and political structure to economic development. They argue that in the "state of nature" at the early stage of economic development, the political system is closed access, which creates rents through the control of the economic barrier to maintain the stability of the political system. Only a few countries developed open access political and economic systems featuring free entry and competition that enable the system to foster long-period economic development. However, they do not explore the mechanism of transition from a closed access to an open access society.

The chapter is structured as follows. The next section introduces a highly stylized model of market expansion decision. Following that, this model is used to simulate the processes of market expansion, deepening of division of labor, and economic growth. We then go on to demonstrate that the decrease of transaction costs and the improvement of factor complementarities are driving forces of economic growth. The numerical simulation of this model not only closely matches our previous discussion of historical facts, but also facilitates a better understanding of certain aspects of China's historical facts. The relationship between market extent and contractual forms is then discussed, following by a brief conclusion.

Market expansion decision and economic growth

Market expansion itself is a consequence of individual decision. Without loss of generality, we consider a CES production function of a representative firm:

$$Y = \left[\sum_{i=1}^{n} \left(\frac{K_i}{n} \right) \alpha \right]^{\frac{1}{\alpha}} \tag{1}$$

Where Y stands for the total output of the firm, n production factors are applied in the production process, representative agent i is positioned in market I, and it owns K_i production factors, it is assumed that n agents act correspondingly to n markets, everyone applies $1/n$ of its total production factors to its production, and the rest are used to exchange production factors complementary to its own with agents in the rest $(n-1)$ markets. To simplify it, we abandoned description of price mechanism, while assuming market exchanges are through barter, the difference only lies in different production factors. In particular, when n equals 1, the n markets are segmented and there is no exchange of factors among the markets, and agents in every market manufacture only with its own production factors. α is the parameter for production function; as a particular case, when α is approaching 1, the production function will degenerate to a linear production function, different production factors can entirely replace each other. When α is approaching 0, the production function tends to be a Cobb Douglas production function. Actually, the production functions mentioned above can be also regarded as utility functions given our simple set-up; then Y is correspondingly regarded as utility, and K_i is considered product consumed by the generic agent i.

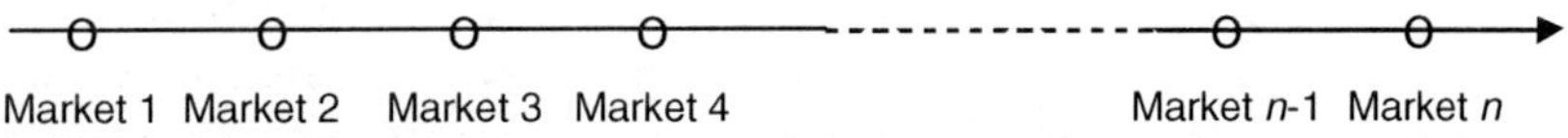

Figure 3.2 A linear city model.

Below, we consider the marginal decision of the representative agent to expand its transaction from the n-th market to the $n+1$-th market. We assume that for agent i, the other $n-1$ agents are evenly distributed in a linear city model, the distance between every two cities is the same (as is shown in Figure 3.2), the transaction cost is a ratio $\beta(0 < \beta < 1)$ of number of transactions, in the sense of iceberg cost à la Samuelson (1954), a reduced form treatment of transaction cost.[1]

With these assumptions, the total cost in exchange between agents in Market 1 and the other $n-1$ markets is

$$\frac{\beta K}{n} + 2\frac{\beta K}{n} + 3\frac{\beta K}{n} + \ldots + (n-1)\frac{\beta K}{n} = \frac{\beta K(n-1)}{n} \tag{2}$$

Therefore, when the market number is n (i.e. n markets trade with each other), net payoff (NY) of agents in Market 1 is

$$NY_n = \left(\sum_{i=1}^{n}\left(\frac{K_i}{n}\right)^{\alpha}\right)^{\frac{1}{\alpha}} - \frac{\beta K_i(n-1)}{2} \tag{3}$$

Correspondingly, if the market scale is $n+1$, then representative agents need to get over n markets to trade, and the net profit is

$$NY_{n+1} = \left(\sum_{i=1}^{n+1}\left(\frac{K_i}{n+1}\right)^{\alpha}\right)^{\frac{1}{\alpha}} - \frac{\beta K_i n}{2} \tag{4}$$

Hence, when the market scale is expanded from n to $n+1$, the margin between the net profit can be written as the difference between function (3) and (4), i.e.

$$\Delta = \left(\sum_{i=1}^{n+1}\left(\frac{K_i}{n+1}\right)^{\alpha}\right)^{\frac{1}{\alpha}} - \left(\sum_{i=1}^{n}\left(\frac{K_i}{n}\right)^{\alpha}\right)^{\frac{1}{\alpha}} - \frac{\beta K_i}{2} \tag{5}$$

When Δ is positive, representative agents will expand the market to the $n+1$-th market; when Δ is negative, representative agents will not.

It is not difficult to show that, when the other parameters are given, the change in factor amount accumulated will lead to change in the value of Δ. A common case is, with the of accumulation of factors, the marginal productivity of factors will decrease, while with the complementary factors from market $n+1$, the marginal productivity can be improved, then the value of Δ can turn from negative to positive, the market scale will be expanded from market $n+1$.

Now we do some comparative statics of the above stylized model. First, let's explore how Δ changes with the accumulation of factors, given the market extent. Differentiating Δ with respect to K, we can get

$$\frac{\partial \Delta}{\partial K_i} = \left(\sum_{i=1}^{n+1}\left(\frac{K_i}{n+1}\right)^{\alpha}\right)^{\left(\frac{1}{\alpha}-1\right)}\left(\frac{K_i}{n+1}\right)^{\alpha-1} - \left(\sum_{i=1}^{n}\left(\frac{K_i}{n}\right)^{\alpha}\right)^{\left(\frac{1}{\alpha}-1\right)}$$
$$\times \left(\frac{K_i}{n}\right)^{\alpha-1} - \frac{\beta}{2} \tag{6}$$

Due to the symmetry of the model, the function above can be reduced to

$$\frac{\partial \Delta}{\partial K_i} = (n+1)^{\frac{1-\alpha}{\alpha}} - n^{\frac{1-\alpha}{\alpha}} - \frac{\beta}{2} \tag{7}$$

Therefore, market extent depends on three variables in the model: substitutability of factors, transaction cost and market size, as discussed below.

Substitutability of factors. With CES production functions, when α is approaching 1, it will degenerate to linear production function and different production factors can completely replace each other. In this case, the value of the above formula is negative. And with accumulation of factors, net profit from new production factors gained from market expansion is negative, while when α is approaching 0, the production function converges to a Cobb Douglas function. In that case, there exists strong complementarity between different market factors, and the decreasing tendency of possible marginal returns of factors in accumulation of factors is likely to be checked by market expansion and obtainment of new complementary production factors. In economic development, the advancement of production technology will lead to change in value of α. Let's imagine that in a farming society, everybody works as the same labor in agriculture production. In this case, the substitutability of different factors is very strong. But in the present knowledge-based economy age, everybody possesses different knowledge, and complementarity between factors is increasingly strong. This means that with economic development, especially with the emergence of a knowledge-based economy, there is increasing complementarity in production and therefore market expansion is playing an increasingly important role in checking the decreasing tendency of marginal returns in accumulation of factors.

Transaction cost. Differentiating the above expression with respect to β leads to a negative result. This proves that a decrease in transaction cost can also help conquer diminishing marginal returns in the accumulation of factors through market expansion.

Market size. Differentiating the above expression with respect to n, we get

$$\frac{\partial^2 \Delta}{\partial K_i \partial n} = \frac{1-\alpha}{\alpha}\left((n+1)^{\frac{1-2\alpha}{\alpha}} - n^{\frac{1-2\alpha}{\alpha}}\right) \qquad (8)$$

It is not hard to find that when $\alpha < 0.5$, complementarity between factors is strong, the value of the above formula is positive. In this case, with larger market size, market expansion is playing an important role in conquering diminishing marginal returns in factors accumulation, and therefore, market size itself will show "increasing returns to scale". While when $0.5 < \alpha < 1$, the value of the above formula is negative. As the complementarity between factors is not strong enough, market expansion is playing a less important role in conquering diminishing marginal returns in factors accumulation, and therefore, market size itself will show "decreasing returns to scale".

Capital accumulation, economic growth and market expansion

We are now in a position to extend the above-mentioned model to a dynamic setting to study the interactions between capital accumulation, economic development and market expansion. First, we can regard the expression of $NY_{n,t}$ as an expression of the net output when the market scale is n in period t, through assumption of a saving ratio (capital accumulation ratio) r, according to (3). We can express the net output in period $t+1$ in condition of unexpanded market as

$$NY_{n,t+1} = \left(\sum_{i=1}^{n}\left(\frac{K_i + rNY_{n,t}}{n}\right)^{\alpha}\right)^{\frac{1}{\alpha}} - \frac{\beta(K_i + rNY_{n,t})(n-1)}{2} \qquad (9)$$

while when the market scale is expanded to $n+1$, according to (4), the net output in period $t+1$ can be expressed as

$$NY_{n+1,t+1} = \left(\sum_{i=1}^{n+1}\left(\frac{K_i + rNY_{n,t}}{n+1}\right)^{\alpha}\right)^{\frac{1}{\alpha}} - \frac{\beta(K_i + rNY_{n,t})n}{2} \qquad (10)$$

Therefore, the motion of economic aggregate can be described by this formula:

$$NY_{t+1} = Max(NY_{n,t+1}, NY_{n+1,t+1}) \qquad (11)$$

Correspondingly, the motion of ecnomic growth rate can be described as

$$G_{t+1} = \frac{NY_{t+1} - NY_t}{NY_t} \qquad (12)$$

The interaction between capital accumulation, economic development and market expansion with numerical simulation can be described to make it more intuitive.

In the simulation, we assign $\alpha = 0.7$; $\beta = 0.1$; $r = 0.2$. With these parameter values, we can get the generic result. Therefore, we focus on the result shown in Figure 3.3. In the simulation, we assign the initial value of K and n both 1; that is, we are simulating an economy developing from a single market without any factors exchanged, in which the initial stock of the factors is standardized at 1. The simulation results obtained are shown in Figure 3.3.

The top left corner shows the tendency of the fluctuation of economy over time, and the horizontal axis stands for time and the vertical axis stands for economic aggregate. It can be inferred that, generally speaking, the aggregate economic activity is becoming increasingly big in economic development. In the process of economic development, factor accumulation and deepened division of labor brought by market expansion are the two main driver forces. The top right corner shows the time tendency of economic growth rate. It is interesting to note that the economic growth rate firstly drops, then rises and eventually stabilizes. This can be explained as follows. Economic growth is driven by two main factors. The first is factor accumulation: the law of marginal returns of factors will set in and economic growth rate will diminish as well. The second is market expansion: as new complementary production factors are introduced (by technological innovation), the diminishing marginal returns can be checked by market expansion. However, the expansion of the market cannot continue forever, since we assume that market expansion is linear. And transaction cost caused by market expansion is increasingly costly and the expansion of the market will be limited to a certain extent. In our simulation result, period 28 is a threshold. Before period 28, market scale grows by 1 each period, while after period 28, market expansion stops at period 29 (see bottom left corner). Here, although economy is still growing, its growth rate remains the same, simulation result is 0.397 (see the top right corner). The bottom right figure shows the change of ratio of total transaction cost to net output. It is very interesting that as markets expand, the ratio is also growing and this tendency will stop as market expansion stops. In terms of service sector in the, interpreted as transition cost at large, then the ratio is increasing with economic development. And this is consistent with the empirical findings (North and Wallis 1986).

Transaction cost, factor complementarity and growth: the past and the present

That market expansion will stop at some time; is it possible to break this deadlock to sustain the market expansion and keep the growth rate? The answer is positive. In the model presented here, the main barrier for market expansion is transaction cost, and the marginal transaction cost is increasing with growth of market scale. If the unit transaction cost can be decreased, sustained market expansion and sustained growth are possible. There are many ways that unit transaction cost can be decreased. One example is transactions having scale economy: the more people are involved in the transaction, the lower the unit transaction cost, given fixed transaction costs. Besides, it can also be interpreted that when the

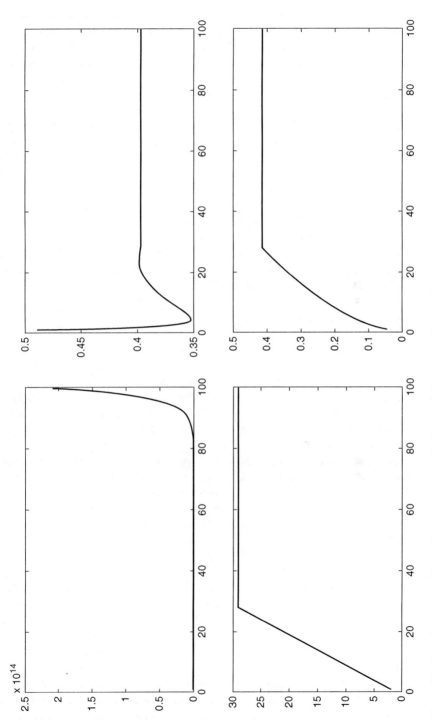

Figure 3.3 Growth pattern without changes in transaction cost and factor complementarity.

market expands, transaction technologies themselves such as communication technologies develop. In Figure 3.4, we assume unit transaction cost β is no longer constant and decreases as market expands. In the simulation, we get the following form:

$$\beta_{t+1} = \beta_t - 0.01/(100 - n_{t+1}) \tag{13}$$

Comparing simulation results in Figures 3.3 and 3.4, we can see that with a constant drop in unit transaction cost, the economic growth rate can be sustained (see top right corner). And at the same time, the market expansion can be sustained (see bottom left corner). Changes in the ratio of total transaction costs are also very interesting: when the market expands, this ratio is rising, while when the market stops expanding, this rate drops to some degree. As a general trend, this rate only slightly rises after period 29.

As mentioned above, market expansion and economic development themselves can also lead to change in production technology. Complementarity of factors is constantly strengthened in this process and this can sustain market expansion. Figure 3.5 simulates the impact of strengthened factor complementarity on market scale and economic development. In our simulation, the change of factor complementarity takes the following form:

$$\alpha_{t+1} = \alpha_t - 0.01/(100 - n_{t+1}) \tag{14}$$

Results of the simulation show that, due to decreasing unit transaction cost and increasing factor complementarity, market expansion and economic growth both accelerate. Meanwhile, the ratio of the total transaction costs to total output demonstrates more obvious upward trend, as shown in Figure 3.4.

The simulation results are surprisingly consistent with human history. First, we found that per capita economic aggregate shows a very similar pattern to the world economic history (Figure 3.1): ancient economic growth occurred very slowly, while modern economic growth is rapid. Second, the simulation result of market expansion can shed some light on the formation of nation-states and economic globalization. We find that in every numerical simulation figure there is a sharp kink in the bottom left corner. This shows that in the process of economic development, there is a natural threshold, before which the market expands very quickly, while after which, market expansion comes to halt. At this point, economic development will be driven only by capital accumulation, if there is no decreasing transaction cost and increasing factor complementarity (as shown in Figure 3.3). Therefore, we can regard this threshold as the efficient boundary of a national economy.[2] Moreover, decreasing unit transaction cost and increasing factor complementarity are the driving forces for economic globalization. And if we regard the service sector as the sector generating transaction costs, then the ratio of service sector rises in economic development. Its maximum ratio in total social output is at around 0.4 (North and Wallis 1986). When we take factor complementarity into account, the ratio might continue to rise.

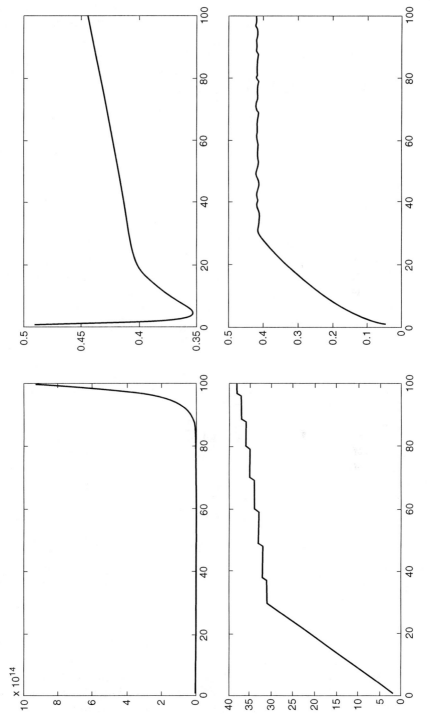

Figure 3.4 Growth pattern with changing transaction cost, keeping factor complementarity constant.

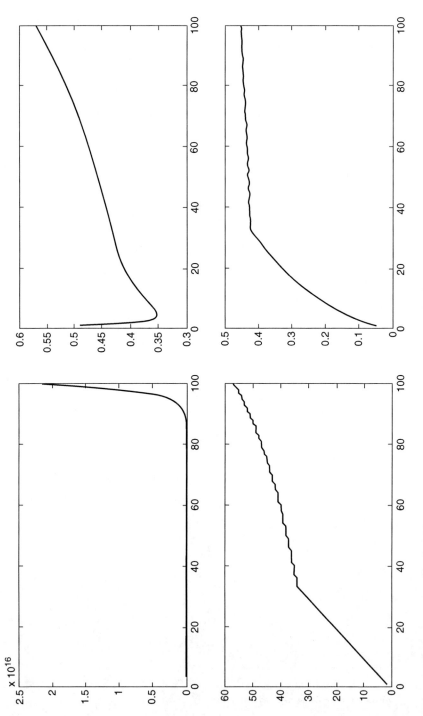

Figure 3.5 Growth pattern with both changing transaction cost and factor complementarity.

Our model can shed some light on Chinese economic history. For students of Chinese economic history, the so-called Needham puzzle (why didn't the industrial revolution originate in China?) is an intriguing topic. There are many plausible explanations. For instance, Lin (1995) argues that Chinese innovation was based on experience after the fourteenth century. The experience-based innovation model was suitable for China then, given the large size of the Chinese population and the law of large numbers. When it comes to modern times, technological innovations depend crucially on scientific methods and experimental tests. Thus Europe (especially after the scientific revolution in the eighteenth century) draws ahead. The simulation in this chapter can help us to understand Chinese history from a new perspective. As is known, the Ming dynasty is a very important turning point in Chinese history. Before that, many Chinese dynasties were open to the outside world. However, in the Ming dynasty and the following Qing dynasty, China adopted a closed door policy. Given the limited market expansion within the closed door policy, economic growth could only depend on capital accumulation. In that condition, we observe the dual phenomena: decreasing marginal factor productivity and growth slowdown in capital accumulation in a closed system, and failure to achieve technologic progress without sufficient complementary factors from other markets.[3] China's economic rise since the late 1970s has also been due to opening up and market expansion.

The future economic development of China largely depends on whether a nationwide free market can emerge to boost economies of scale in China. However, as is observed by many economists, including us, there exists high trade barriers between different provinces in China, which inhibits the formation of a free market across China (Young 2000; Poncet 2003; Lu *et al.* 2004). If such interprovincial barriers cannot be well addressed, China can hardly reap the full benefits of scale economy in its economic growth process.

By way of conclusion: market size, division of labor and contractual forms

This chapter develops an economic model to characterize the selection of market extent. Market expansion can check diminishing returns through factor complementarities or avoid diminishing utility through product complementarities. In this process, economic growth makes market expansion a desired option, while market expansion contributes to faster economic growth. The numerical simulation results derived from this model not only shed some light on global economic history, but also account for the history and reality of Chinese economy. With market expansion and deeper specialization, rule-based contracts are more important for compensating *ex post* loss in market expansion. This theory is essentially a development theory, in which market expansion, deeper specialization, economic growth and evolution of contractual forms represent dimensions of the development process.

This chapter can offer a starting point for further research, for example along the following lines. (1) Linear spatial models were adopted here, while future research may employ circle models that are closer to reality. (2) Transaction costs remain a black box in this chapter, but a possible path of further study may be an investigation of the internal relations between market scale, economic growth and contractual forms by characterizing the relationship between division of labor and market interlinkage to obtain a better understanding of strategic interactions between agents across interlinked markets.

As argued in the previous chapter, in the early stage of development, due to limited specialization and missing markets, the same pair of agents more often than not conduct multiple transactions and the transactions are interlinked. However, with expansion of the markets and deeper specialization, an agent will trade with new people in separate transactions and the contractual interlinkage will unravel. A promising future avenue of study would be to look at the relationship between market scale and contractual forms in a growth model where contractual forms arise endogenously.

4 Interlinked contracts and development

Where do we stand?

Interlinked contracts prevail in less developed countries (LDCs). Understanding the rationale, structure and dynamics of such contracts is crucial to a better understanding of economic development and institutional changes and policy-making. This chapter provides a review of the existing theoretical literature, by first setting the stage for interlinked contracts and then by reviewing the theoretical rationale and pros and cons of such contractual interlinkage. The main role of this chapter is to set a theoretical background for the book.

Despite the fact that economists and anthropologists since Lewis (1954) and Polanyi (1957) have come to realize the structural and institutional differences between traditional and modern societies, policy-makers more often than not have taken a simple-minded approach to modernizing agricultural and traditional socioeconomic structures, failing to take full account of the subtle and complex institutional structures in the traditional sector. Throughout the process, the urban market economy has been taken as the blueprint, and market competition introduced ubiquitously. In the policy arena, modern technologies and financial institutions are introduced, and compulsory increases of wage for rural workers or sharecropping ratio are invoked. However, these policies, intended to improve tenants' welfare, more often than not may do the opposite. For instance, economists have observed that in some regions of India landlords and tenants have rejected advanced agricultural technologies because of increased risk to output. Despite the opening of rural credit unions, tenants have continued to borrow money from landlords. This again has led to government subsidies, given to tenants via either land or credit markets, finding their way into the landlords' pockets through either of these channels due to repeat landlord–tenant interactions. As a result, governments' attempts to end interlinked relationships through various regulations have often led to a decline in production and a decrease in tenant welfare (Bhaduri 1973; Bardhan 1980, 1984; Bell 1988).

This phenomenon indicates that there may be some intricate equilibrium contract structure in traditional society that requires careful study The existence of such a structure could be highly consequential in determining whether or not the introduction of modern market institutions is able to deliver the intended results, especially in light of the fact that interlinked contracts are widely present in agricultural economies. This system means that the two parties (be they landlords, tenants, traders of agricultural produce or professional lenders) trade by "bundling" several transactions or contracts (such as tenancy, credit and labor contract). The interlinked contract system has the following characteristics: (1) simultaneity, meaning multiple contracts that would otherwise occur at different times and with different conditions being placed under the same umbrella; (2) transactions being contingent on one another, meaning agreement to one transaction should be conditional on agreement to all other transactions; (3) the interlock/isolation of transactions, where the interlinked contract deepens the relationship between the participating parties, yet simultaneously reduces the interaction of the trading parties with the external environment. This is because interlinked "insiders" tend to employ "discounted" or "preferential" prices, which would constitute a trading impediment to outsiders, rendering trade comparatively isolated from external markets (if any). Some leftists even argue that the "rich" (e.g. the landlord-trader-lender) are able to intensify their exploitation of the "poor" (tenants) through interlinked transactions.

However, further investigation reveals that interlinked contracts may not contribute to exploitation or reduce efficiency. On the contrary, they may improve efficiency in the event of imperfect information and incomplete markets (Bell 1988; Bell and Srinivasan 1989). More counter-intuitively, given that we are in a second-best world, an improvement in some margin could reduce global welfare loss in developing economies with incomplete markets.

In this regard, research on interlinked contracts is of crucial importance for development economics and policies. This chapter aims to delineate the rationales and their economic consequences, drawing some policy implications. The next section presents the socioeconomic background; following that is a description of the efficiency rationales for the emergence of interlinked contracts. Then the limitations and inefficiencies of interlinked contracts (intensive vs extensive margins) are presented; and finally the implications of interlinked contracts for the dynamics of economic development and institutional changes are explored.

Contractual structure in a traditional society

As we have mentioned, due to a lack of specialization and incomplete markets, the transactions of the same pair of persons may be interlinked in traditional societies. Traditional societies are characterized by the following features.

First, the absence of division of labor among the population in traditional agricultural societies leads to the following. (1) One person trades with other people naturally as a provider of multiple products and services. Capital owners are usually also employers, providers of production and consumption credit, and traders and purchasers of agricultural produce. Labor providers, too, play multiple roles, acting as employees, borrowers and sellers of agricultural produce. (2) Without sufficient division of labor, no market with free competition could develop. The limited extent of the market, on the other hand, constrains the deepening of the division of labor. Therefore, personalized transactions are far more pervasive.

Second, the agricultural market features persistent fluctuations and seasonal variations. Thus it is necessary to reduce the risk through certain institutional arrangements. For instance, tenants may have to depend on borrowing for sustenance during the crop-growing season, while it may be difficult for landlords and grain traders to find sufficient available labor and physical good supplies during the harvest season. Their demand is almost inelastic at certain points in time. It is thus necessary to smooth such fluctuations through some special forward-like transaction.

Third, with the exception of future labor and grain outputs, most tenants do not have enough assets to use as collateral for loans. This means that they must sign loan contracts for the delivery of services and physical goods in the future. As tenants have different potential labor supplies and production capacities in the future, signing multiple contracts will help lenders obtain the inside information that would otherwise be unavailable. Such interlinked contracts also have economies of scale in terms of information collection: information about a borrower contained in one contract with the lender can potentially uncover related information contained elsewhere.

Fourth, agricultural production faces greater moral hazard than some of its industrial counterparts. This is because the heterogeneity and risk of agricultural production can make it hard for the person involved to distinguish the results of shirking from the results of exogenous shock. The usual performance evaluation is not applicable to incentives for tenants, while the sharecropping system of single transactions could at most lead to a sub-optimal arrangement in terms of risk and incentive. Under such conditions, incentives for tenants provided by other transactions may lead to Pareto improvement.

Fifth, traditional societies generally lack well-established infrastructures such as advanced transportation and information systems. This means that excessively high transaction costs for tenants to travel to various locations place high premiums on extra-territorial transactions. In contrast, bundling several transactions together can substantially lower transaction costs.

In summary, given the low division of labor, the various market imperfections, and the technology and the trading environments of rural society, the pattern of "separate transactions" is infeasible and unenforceable. Bundling several transactions across "markets" and time periods can lead to Pareto improvement by decreasing transaction costs, satisfying time preference, and providing extra information and incentives. Next, the economic rationales for and the advantages of interlinked contracts are explored based on the existing literature.

The rationale and advantages of interlinked contracts

Research into interlinked contracts goes back at least to Bhaduri (1973). The field was subsequently expanded, with studies by Bell and Zusman (1976), Bardhan (1980, 1984), Mitra (1982), Braverman and Stiglitz (1982), Basu (1983, 1984) and Bell (1988), among others. They demonstrate the rationales and roles of the interlinked contract in the traditional rural society, and study the related trade-offs. This section focuses on the rationales and advantages of interlinked contracts.

Traditional society and transaction costs

During the 1980s, interlinked contract theory mainly tried to interpret market interlinkage in the traditional agricultural economy through various types of "transaction costs". Considering the insufficient monetization and low labor market mobility of the agricultural economy, it was believed that it would be difficult for tenants to repay loans in the future under insufficient monetary income constraints. At the same time, it was also difficult for landlords to act as urban capitalists and employ a large enough labor force during harvest time via the free labor market. Thus, interlinked markets emerged as "double coincidence of wants", and "barter" developed in the case of insufficient monetization. Therefore, the "personalized transaction" between landlords and tenants reduced various transaction costs, such as monitoring costs, enforcement costs and search cost among others. Further, this kind of interlinked contract could be Pareto improving.

Bardhan (1980) notes that the interlinkage of tenancy-credit contracts corresponds to the context of low monetization, in which the tenant uses his income in the future as collateral to obtain the acceptance of the employer-lender or the landlord, and at the same time, also guarantees a special arrangement of labor supply during harvest period for the landlord. This could be regarded as a kind of "barter" involving multiple goods. Bell (1988) uses the same example to show that although sufficient monetization may produce the effective arrangement that tenants could sign loan contracts during the non-harvest period based on market prices, and landlords could employ labor based on market prices, the two parties in these two types of transactions would have to enter into very complicated contracts dependent on the trading environment and on their respective bargaining powers. This would surely increase the costs of the two parties. However, if the two contracts were bundled, this would at least reduce the search and enforcement costs.

Empirical studies support the theoretical predictions. Research on rural villages in India by Sarap (1991) shows that if a poor villager wanted to obtain a loan from a credit institution, their travel cost may account for 5 to 10 percent of the locally obtained loan, due to the small size of the loans and extremely inconvenient transport in rural areas. It naturally follows that in the face of such high transaction costs, tenants would not be interested even when presented with "separate contracting" opportunities. Relative to the small size of the loans, even tiny transaction costs could also render the "real interest rates" of rural credit unions much higher than the nominal interest rates. Thus, "localized" interlinked transactions have big advantages: as long as the interest rates of the "usurious loans" are not higher than the sum of the interest rates of the credit unions and the associated transaction costs, tenants will find the terms attractive.

Information asymmetry and screening

Under the "interlinked contract" framework, economists have applied the screening theory mainly to explain the following phenomena present in agriculture and rural economics. (1) Laws and regulations regarding contractual enforcement in traditional agricultural society are not developed, so it should be of low probability that tenants "defaulting on loans" could be caught and effectively punished. In other words, the cost of "evading loan repayment" for a tenant is very low. (2) Despite the lack of a formal legal structure, the default rate in rural societies is extremely low. So there must be certain effective contract enforcement mechanisms.

Basu (1983) uses a descriptive model to show that landlords in the agricultural economy always have a certain degree of control over the tenants working on their farms, but they have much less control over those tenants who borrow money from them. Therefore, in the absence of collateral for tenants' loans, the feasible loan contracts would be those between the landlords and their tenants. This model offers an interpretation for the emergence of the "interlinked contract" in rural markets. Since the landlords are always able to control tenants through a contract linking interest rates and wages, they would optimally choose a combination of interest rate and wages to maximize their benefits. By keeping tenants at their reservation utility level, landlords would trade off between the interest rate margin and the wage margin. Furthermore, a low interest rate and low wage combination is better than high interest rate and high wage combination. This is true because lower interest rates would attract more tenants to borrow, and the interlinked contract enhances the means and possibilities for landlords to improve their own welfare while keeping the tenants' welfare at the reservation level, shifting the social welfare possibility frontier outward, which is a Pareto improving arrangement.[1]

Allen (1985) applies a more formal model to show that for potential loan providers (landlords), the land tenancy provides more information about the repayment capability of the tenants. As has been shown by the research on sharecropping, more risk-loving agents will choose fixed rent contracts, while risk-averse agents prefer fixed wage or sharecropping contracts. If tenants with high repayment capabilities also withstand risks better, it could be deduced that those who sign fixed rent contracts are agents with high capabilities, and that loans with high interest rates and large principals could be offered to them. For tenants choosing sharecropping contracts, loans with small principals and low interest rates could be offered, thereby achieving maximum interest rate income and minimum loan default. Both of the above predictions seem to be supported by empirical research. For instance, a survey on the Punjab region in India by Bell, Srinivasan and Udry (1997) shows that introducing clauses related to product sharing and grain sale into loan contracts could significantly increase the amount that informal lenders are willing to lend.

Banerji (1995) uses an agency model with different time preferences to explain the emergence of interlinked contracts, arguing that the interlinked contract is a second-best arrangement. Time preference reflects the patience of the agents, where agent A has a high degree of patience and agent B a low degree of patience. (1) For the same loan interests, A asks for a lower sharecropping ratio in the future than B (A values income in the future more than B, and so for the same cost, he needs less income in the future as compensation). (2) For the same increases of sharecropping ratios, A is willing to shoulder more interest increases (willing to offer higher prices for income in the future) than B. The output is determined by the capital invested by the agent in the first period. Higher sharecropping ratios imply a higher return to capital. Therefore, higher sharecropping ratios would certainly bring more capital investment and more output. The model shows that the best contract design is to make the incentive constraint for A binding, and that for B non-binding. As a consequence, the sharecropping ratio for B is lower than the optimal level, thus leading to insufficient investment. This is all due to contractual interlinkage between the interest rates and sharecropping ratios; the resultant low efficiency is attributable the interlinked contract.

Despite these theoretical insights, the above literature is lacking in extensive follow-up research. The reason may be that many assumptions of the adverse selection model actually do not conform to the practical realities of interlinked contracts. For instance, the information in an agricultural society is not as insufficient as was assumed. Actually, in a small community, landlords can have various channels through which they can get to know the backgrounds of tenants. This indicates that adverse selection is not a suitable model to study interlinked contracts. On the contrary, moral hazard model may be a better candidate for the study.

Monitoring, technology and distribution in agricultural production and the moral hazard model

Braverman and Stiglitz (1982) were among the first to formally study interlinked contracts in the context of sharecropping with moral hazard. They show that linking credit contracts to tenancy can enhance tenants' production efforts. They assume the production function $Y = gf(e)$, where g is a random coefficient, representing the impact on the production by nature, and $f_e > 0$ represents production as an increasing function of tenants' effort input. The utilities of the landlord and tenant are determined by the sharecropping share specified in the tenancy contract, and the loan amount and interest rates stipulated in the loan contract. Here we set a sharecropping coefficient α, and assume that for output $Y_0 = g_0 f(e_0)$, tenants could achieve the ratio αY_0, and that landlords get $(1 - \alpha)Y_0$; we also assume that the loan amount is B and interest rate is r, the tenants' initial wealth is W_0, then the tenants' consumptions during the two periods are determined by $c_0 = W_0 + B, c_1 = \alpha Y - (1 + r)B$. In the first period, the landlord offers loan B, and his income in the second period is $\bar{P} = (1 - \alpha)Y + (1 + r)B$. Since the income of the two individuals in the first period have nothing to do with effort e, we will focus on the issue of optimization during the second period.

In the second period, the tenant faces an expected utility function $EU(c_1, e)$, where EU increases with c_1 and e affects expected utility in two ways: the disutility makes the partial derivative of EU with respect to e negative, and the production Y_0 increases with e. The core of the argument lies in the negative relationship between B and $c_1 : c_1 = \alpha Y - (1+r)B$. With concave utility function ($U_{c_1 c_1} < 0$), and $U_{ec_1} < 0$, that is, the disutility of labor increases with the consumption level c_1. Since the tenant's income is always kept at the level of reservation utility, the increased effort finally transforms into increased profit for the landlord. In conclusion, this model offers quite a good explanation of why interlinked contracts prevail in the rural economy: the coupling of loan and tenancy contracts mitigates moral hazard problems in the tenancy contract and improves efficiency.

In light of this insight, we analyze the effects of contractual details on incentives and efficiency: in particular, the effect of the default clause and bonded labor clause. The default clause specifies the limited liability for the loan contract, and the landlord guarantees the lowest "reservation" consumption $\hat{c}$ for the tenant. If the tenant's income, with the lowest consumption $\alpha Y - \hat{c}$ deducted, is not enough for repaying the debts owed to the landlord, then the difference would not be repaid. The bonded labor clause specifies the extra labor of the tenant in case he cannot repay the loan, and the landlord may have the right to turn the tenant into a slave.

The above analysis has two implications for the agricultural economy. (1) In terms of effort incentives, the default clause would make the tenant's utility consumption curve more flat while the bonded labor contract would act the other way round. In terms of marginal effect, the bonded labor clause would provide more incentive than the default clause; regarding the relation between the loan size B and the effort e, the larger the loan, the higher the possibility that the tenant will default (fall into bonded labor, respectively) under the default clause (bonded labor clause, respectively). The higher defaults (bonded labor, respectively) possibility would always provide less effort (more effort, respectively) incentives, and higher loan size B would mean less effort (more effort, respectively) and lower efficiency (higher efficiency, respectively) under the default/bonded labor clauses. (2) In terms of technology risk, the default clause reduces the risks undertaken by the tenant, while the bonded labor clause increases the tenant's risks, and makes them reluctant to use more efficient but riskier technology. It can be shown that the larger the size of the loan, the higher the possibility that the tenant will default and fall into bonded labor clauses. We know that the optimal technology choice is directly proportional to the absolute risk aversion degree $A \equiv -\frac{U_{cc}}{U_c}$. It is obvious that the bonded labor clause would increase U_c and further reduce optimal risk taking. And though the default clause is not good for incentives, it makes the tenant more willing to apply newer and more risky technology because it provides him with extra protection.

Mitra (1983) further analyzes how a flexible adjustment of interlinked contracts responds to external changes. He argues that the cancellation of an interlinked contract would not only undermine the incentives for the tenant, it would also force the landlord to reduce the sharecropping ratio and wages and loans for the tenant, undermining the latter's welfare. With a model similar to that of Braverman and Stiglitz (1982), Mitra shows that the existence of an interlinked contact would promote efficiency by providing extra effort incentive for the tenant. His comparative static analysis demonstrates: (1) the increase in reservation utility (e.g. wage level on the external markets); (2) the opening up of external credit markets and the decrease of interest rates; and (3) the application of new technology leading to either a decrease or an increase of production variance.

Through comparative statics Mitra concludes that in order to increase the reservation utility $\bar{u}$, the optimal adjustment by the landlord to an interlinked contract should be to increase the loan size c,[2] reduce the loan interest rate ti (i is the interest rate of the external market, t is an increase or decrease coefficient provided by the landlord based on the basic interest rate) and adjust the values of α and β depending on risk aversion σ. The intuition is as follows. The increase of reservation utility means that the landlord needs to offer more favorable conditions to the tenant. However, the coefficient in the sharecropping contract must be dependent on values of σ: when σ is quite large (small, respectively), and α decreases (increases, respectively) as $\bar{u}$ increases. In the usual moral hazard sharecropping models, a large σ means the agent's risk aversion degree is high. Therefore, the insurance is quite important: a higher fixed wage α and a lower sharecropping ratio β should be provided. However, here we don't solve for the value of α, but the response of α to the change of $\bar{u}$. When $\bar{u}$ increases, the total consumption level C must increase; the larger the σ is, the more quickly the marginal utility from the consumption would diminish. The tenant has no incentive to exert greater effort for more income. Therefore, σ actually changes from a risk-sharing measure in the normal moral hazard model into an incentive indicator. The bigger σ is, the more serious the incentive margin will be (*ceteris paribus*), and the more important it will be to increase the sharecropping ratio β and reduce the fixed wage α when the reservation utility $\bar{u}$ increases.

Since σ here is actually an incentive instrument rather than an insurance instrument, the following prediction is straightforward: when σ is large, an increase in the interest rate on the open market could incentivize the landlord to reduce the loan size c and the fixed wage α for the tenant, keeping landlord's mark-up coefficient t constant. The intuition here is that, similar to increasing the tenant's income, decreasing the interest rate would reduce the tenant's incentive. Also the landlord may further reduce losses from the interest rate decrease by reducing the sharecropping ratio β, assuming the incentive problem is not serious. Therefore, this proposition actually indicates that, *ceteris paribus*, the sudden introduction of external credit markets or rural credit subsidies into the agricultural economy may lead to unintended consequences: the benefit that the tenants could obtain is very limited, and their actual income may decrease due to reduced sharecropping portion in one margin and reduced wages in the other margin.

In summary, in the moral hazard model, the landlord can structure the tenant's work incentive and choice of technology by manipulating the contract clauses (including the default clause and the bonded labor clause). The interlinked contract provides the tenant with more insurance when the insurance margin matters in order to incentivize the tenant to adopt new technologies; when the incentive margin matters more, increasing default punishment will enhance their work incentive. Both will increase efficiency. This should be taken into account in policy-making. A reform aimed at improving the tenant's welfare may turn out to be inefficient, as the intended effects might be undone by a reduction of the tenant's share of income by the landlord.

The effects of competition among lenders

One popular concern is that interlinked contracts may enhance landlords' monopoly and undermine competition. However, when competition among potential principals is introduced into the model, the interlinkage does not reduce competition among lenders.

Ray and Sengupta (1989) and Basu, Bell and Bose (2000) study the relation between interlinkage and competition. The former mainly consider the economic environment where no specialized lenders exist and where lender-landlord and trader-lenders would utilize their respective professional advantages, leading to competition with similar effects to specialization within impersonal markets. The studies assume that tenants are heterogeneous, and that they have the same production function $y = F(K, L)$ and a different capital endowment K. This leads to two differences: one is that tenants with more endowment K have higher marginal productivity MPL, and the other is that K can be used to repay the debts. In a bad state of the world, tenants with higher K would have lower default rates due to higher incomes and wealth. And the lenders with specialized functions work differently at this time: landlords can impose extra punishment on tenants through tenancy contracts while traders cannot do this. Therefore, for tenants with lower K, landlords have stronger control to enhance their effort incentive in order to avoid punishment; on the other hand, because the sharecropping ratio in the tenancy contracts is fixed,[3] landlords still only get the specified sharecropping ratio when tenants with a higher K value have significantly higher output. Traders could capture almost all of these benefits by manipulating product prices (lowering buying prices or increasing selling prices) if they have enough market power. Although this is harmful to tenants' welfare, it may produce certain incentive effects[4] and promote production.

From another perspective, Basu, Bell and Bose (2000) show that when there are both interlinked lenders and non-interlinked lenders in a market, the interlinked lenders can still obtain extra advantages through the seniority of claims and the information advantages of state-contingent contracts.[5] This model is about the competition in itself. However, it could also be interpreted as follows: when a lender can "choose" whether to be an interlinked lender or a non-interlinked lender, choosing to be an interlinked lender could offer a maximum guarantee for his benefits. Paradoxically, this may imply that the interlinkage may not suppress competition; rather it may be a result of competition in informal markets.

The above literature collectively demonstrates the rationale of the interlinked contract given the absence of some markets. As shown in the well-known Greenwald and Stiglitz theorem (1986), there can be Pareto improving interventions when the markets are incomplete. The above-mentioned specific models of interlinked contracts can be deemed as particular cases of the theory. Next, we turn to the limitations of interlinked contracts.

Limitations of interlinked contracts

When markets are incomplete, interlinked contracts can promote efficiency through screening potential borrowers. All of these are the primary reasons why interlinked contracts emerge and prevail in traditional society. However, in the process of economic development and completion of markets, the interlinkage can unravel as the economy develops and the division of labor deepens. However, the interlinkage itself may hinder the market expansion and the economic development in the first place.

The conflict between interlinked contracts and technology: between production possibility frontier (PPF) and utility possibility frontier (UPF)

The interlinked contract on the tenancy-loan margins may render landlords (more) unwilling to use technology, which would increase tenants' welfare and total output, at a disadvantage for themselves. Also, landlords tend to use some technology that would increase their own welfare and reduce tenants' welfare and total output. This is a point made clear in the study of the tenancy contract and agricultural technology adoption by Braverman and Stiglitz (1986). They study the adverse impacts of sharecropping tenancy on technical advances given tenancy-loan linkage and how the loan margin may complicate this.

This section first uses a simple method to define technical advance: the outward shift of the marginal production curve, which means that for the original production function $f(e)$ with diminishing marginal return, the new $\hat{f}(e)$ will always produce more output y with the same effort, while at the same output level, it requires less effort e. But it should be noted that the outward shift of the marginal product curve does not always equate to the outward shift of the total output. It is due to the fact that wages are like inferior goods; thus, when the marginal product increases, tenants may turn to pursue more leisure, causing the increase in the marginal output to be offset or even exceeded by a sharp effort decrease. Thus, landlords may not employ such technologies which increase productivity and tenants' welfare.

On the other hand, in order to maximize their own interests, landlords may apply some technologies that are not favorable to tenants' welfare and productivity increase, or which may even be harmful to the total output. This is demonstrated as follows. Suppose the landlord can renegotiate with the tenant, particularly on the sharecropping ratio, and he can keep the tenant's welfare at the reservation level, as in the typical moral hazard model. Thus, a "bad" technology (technology that decreases productivity) could be adopted by the landlord in the following way: the landlord is able to increase his own income by increasing tenants' efforts and reducing the tenants' sharecropping ratios.

Land price, rural labor market and income distribution

The interlinked institutional arrangement may intensify the income disparity and poverty in rural society through the following two channels: (1) under the condition of changing technologies, due to different endowments, the interlinked contract may make tenants more vulnerable to a loss of their land and more dependent on landlords; (2) in the general equilibrium, the interlinkage may entail the adjustment of the land size by landlords for each tenant. Then, given the total land, there must be a fluctuation in the labor market for tenants. Especially when the linkage adjustment usually leads to an increase in the land size, it can increase the income of the participating tenant vis-à-vis the unemployed tenants.

The inequality of income existing in traditional society has not only constituted a severe and long-term problem, it has impeded technological progress. Braverman and Stiglitz (1989) point out that in a traditional sharecropping system, keeping rural residents' income at a relatively low level suggests the existence of landlord exploitation. However, it is a second-best world given the serious information problems. In no way does it mean that trapping rural residents in long-term poverty is the only way to keep them working. They show that turning tenants into yeomen can increase their income and welfare, as well as contribute to improving productivity, because redistributing land to tenants amounts to raising their share in the sharecropping system to 100 percent. Two effects are involved here: (1) tenants will work harder due to the substitution effect between work and leisure; and (2) tenants choose to enjoy more leisure owing to the income effect. Provided that tenants' marginal utilities do not diminish too fast,[6] the substitution effect will outweigh the income effect. Therefore, tenants will go the extra mile and adopt advanced technology to enhance productivity. It is argued, therefore, that any reform that reduces the inequality of land distribution (e.g. turning tenants into yeomen) will enhance productivity in the long term; while those that increase the inequality of land distribution (e.g. turning yeomen into tenants) will impede productivity.

Some implications can be drawn about the effects of technology on land inequality. In the production process, landlords possess plenty of capital and employed labor, while yeomen possess labor but no capital. Assuming we can regard the value of a piece of land as the discounted present value of the long-term output, in a situation where the introduction of new technology increases the contribution of capital to output while decreasing the labor ratio, the value of the landlord's land output is greater than that of peasant's due to his capital advantage. In this case, the landlord has a higher "evaluation" of the land than that of the yeoman, and in a rural land market the price of the supplier (yeoman) decreases while that of the demand side (landlord) increases. This consequently pushes up the transaction volume and transfers more land from yeomen to the landlords, harming development in the long run.

Along these lines, interlinked contracts provide not only consumer credit but also production credit in the sharecropping system. This produces two effects. First, under the new technology,[7] yeomen may acquire capital through the credit market to enhance the land's value without having to sell their land. Second, participation in interlinked contracts themselves requires yeomen to become tenants, which harms their incentives to work. In light of this, the emergence of interlinked contracts may affect the land distribution in two ways and further affect market productivity. (1) Peasants can choose diversification by keeping a piece of land for their own farming and at the same time rent a piece of land to enter into the sharecropping system; this seems quite common in rural economies. That is to say, many peasants have their own land, but they also work on the landlords' land regularly to gain wages, credits and other benefits, which makes the relationship of both parties more complicated.[8] (2) On the other hand, the landlord may exert influence on the yeoman through interlinked contracts and try to acquire his land by any means. What's more, even without purchasing the peasant's land, the landlord can covertly exploit the output from the peasant's land through interlinked contracts. Besides, the tenancy relationship allows the landlord to obtain more information about the income and the output of the peasant. Therefore, once the peasant goes into bankruptcy and has to sell his land, the landlord obtains extra information and negotiation advantage and can even buy the peasant's land at a discount, which worsens the peasant's situation, exacerbates income inequality and attenuates productivity.

In their classic study, Braverman and Stiglitz (1982) discuss the effects of interlinked contracts in partial equilibrium, and also analyze the effect in general equilibrium. Assuming that agricultural production requires both labor and land, and also assuming that for the maximization of profit, the landlord increases the credit B to the peasant while keeping the sharecropping ratio at a fixed value α, then to make sure that the peasant pays back the borrowed money or that the peasant's income minus the minimum consumption is greater than the loan value, the landlord has to raise the peasant's income through increasing the area of leased land. Under the condition that the total land area is fixed, the demand for agricultural laborers decreases, triggering unemployment within the agricultural economy. This process may improve the circumstances of those employed peasants, but at the same time aggravates the welfare loss of unemployed peasants.

A bargaining approach to interlinked contracts

So far our discussion has generally followed the classical principal-agent model. This model assumes that the landlord possesses bargaining power, so that he can propose a take-it-or-leave-it contract, and keep the peasants' utility at the reservation level, which in most cases is in conformity with the current state of the countryside. However, economists sometimes observe that the relationship between landlord and tenant shows more "equality" than the principal-agent model assumes. For example, Bell and Zusman (1976) observe that spring farming can't be done without some non-tradable production factors, like managerial skills, farming tools and animal power, but the landlord himself can't provide all the factors, which implies that tenants need to equip themselves with these factors in order to proceed with the work. Also, this makes the relationship between landlord and tenant similar to one of "bilateral monopoly". In this case, since the interaction between both parties is not replaceable, a bargaining model like that of Nash, which maximizes the sum of both parties' benefits and divides benefits equally among them, can better characterize their relationship, given long-term interactions.

Motivated by the 50:50 sharing rule prevalent in the northern part of India, Bell and Zusman (1976) use a cooperative game approach with various parameters and find that all the results are close to 50:50 profit sharing. Given the fact that Nash bargaining is used to maximize total social welfare, at first glance, this conclusion seems to provide a bright future for improving agricultural efficiency and tenant welfare: we just need to empower the tenant and turn the landlord-tenant relationship into a Nash bargaining relationship. However, if the 50:50 profit-sharing method prevalent in India has already embodied the equal relationship between landlord and tenant of Nash bargaining, we should have seen that facing any new technology innovation, landlord and tenant in India should spontaneously participate in activities that enhance productivity and promote both parties' welfare. However, this situation has not transpired.

Therefore, this line of literature on bargaining sheds some light on improving the status quo, namely how raising the bargaining power of tenants may improve efficiency. But for an agricultural economy full of interlinking relationships, this process of improvement could be rather difficult, and the best description is the example mentioned by Bell (1988): in most cases, a landlord still holds a dominant position in the transaction and the existence of the interlinking relationship strengthens his monopoly power. This is because the peasant can still ask for a wage increase through activities such as strikes without being involved in an interlinked relationship, but those peasants who have borrowed from the landlords dare not voice their protest. This compels us to ponder whether, although the interlinked contract meets the requirement of maximizing the economic value in a static condition, it is worthwhile in the long term to maintain this arrangement at the expense of both social equality and economic efficiency.

Concluding remarks: development and dynamics of interlinked relational contracts

The above literature on interlinked contracts takes place largely in a static setting. In this regard, Wang (2007) proposes a theory of the "interlinked relational contract" and studies in a relational setting, which is particularly suitable for analyzing the dynamics of economic development and institutional change. The core of the theory could be summarized as follows: effective contractual or governance mode is a function of market extent. In developing economies with missing markets and low specialization, the second-best arrangement in response to incomplete markets between economic agents may take the form of interlinked and relational contracts, as highlighted by the aforementioned literature on interlinked contracts. As discussed above, in the agriculture sector of developing economies, landlords and tenants not only trade on the product market (e.g. tenants would purchase grain from landlords), they also interact on the labor market (landlords employ tenants), the credit market (landlords provide credit to tenants) and the insurance market (e.g. the sharecropping renting system). In contrast, in economies with a higher level of division of labor, people would trade with different agents on different specialized markets. Also, since there is almost no need to incur fixed costs in establishing the formal legal system, transaction costs could be greatly reduced.[9] However, as the economy develops and markets become more complete, the governance cost of relational contracts would gradually rise. The completion of the market would itself reduce the contractual interlinkage and relationality (e.g. long-term interaction) through specialization and market thickness effects, which would then cause the relational contract to unravel. At this point, the formal system depending on a third party (e.g. democracy and the rule of law) would help realize greater scale economies. But as Kranton (1996) points out, both the relational contract and impersonal market equilibrium can be self-sustainable. Therefore, some economies can be trapped in some equilibrium for a long time.

The literature on interlinked contracts has come a long way and can shed some light on the relationship between economic development and institutional changes. In particular, an implication is that some institutions are endogenous in their development processes. Therefore, development policies need to address the fundamental causes of some development problems and subtle contractual interlinkage and general equilibrium must be taken into account. The same holds true for transition economies like China, as elaborated in Chapter 5.

5 Unraveling the Chinese miracle

A perspective of interlinked relational contracts

It has been more than 30 years since the beginning of China's reform and opening up. Since 1978 great changes have taken place in China's economy and society. From an international perspective, China's transition is undoubtedly a huge success when compared either with other transition economies like Russia, or with other developing economies. It is an intriguing challenge for social scientists to offer some theory to account for this economic miracle.

A fundamental question we need to answer is what kind of microeconomic mechanism led to the success at the initial stages of the gradual transition. Will this microeconomic mechanism still act as an enabler or turn into an inhibitor for further development of the transition process? Put another way, it is essential that we understand microeconomic foundations and mechanisms underlying the gradual transition in order to have a full analysis of the benefits and costs of the transition.

Widely accepted ideas concerning China's transition and the Russian model include a decentralization theory based on the new soft budget constraint theory à la Dewatripont and Maskin (1995) and an explanation on the basis of the theory of Multi-division Organization Structure and Unitary Organizational Structure. The basic point of this strand of literature is that economic structure (i.e. the degree of decentralization and organizational structure of the whole economy) accounts for the enormous difference in the economic performance of China and Russia during transition: in China, the decentralization reform not only hardened the budget constraint of state-owned enterprises (SOEs), it fostered inter-jurisdictional yardstick competition. This in turn provided effective information about the relative performance of local governments to the central government. Multi-division economic structure also allowed for institutional experimentations in certain chosen regions, without disrupting the whole economy. In contrast, there is no such economic structure in Russia.

The above theory may explain why there has been a big gap between China's and Russia's economic performance during the period of transition. However, the theory does not address the pace of reforms, and cannot explain the more general question as to why gradual reform has achieved better economic performance than radical reform and what is meant by gradualism in the first place. In particular, the theory fails to explain the paradox that since reform and opening up China has sustained a high growth rate without adequate institutional infrastructure, like a sound legal system, well-defined property rights, and an efficient financial system.

Contractual enforcement is essential in any society to get incentives right, especially for a transition economy. In such an economy, institutions and social norms governing economic activities have recently undergone enormous change, which make it more difficult to enforce contracts and honor commitments. To a large extent, different political, economic and social structures have different mechanisms of contract enforcement. Decentralization (fiscal federalism) constitutes a credible commitment device in the political system, but the same issue has not been tackled in the economic and social structures. Since all these are usually highly related to one another, we can hardly understand them if each is studied in isolation.

The purpose of this chapter is to provide a theoretical framework from the perspective of contract enforcement to lay down the socioeconomic foundations of China's economic transition. The next section presents a theory of interlinked relational contracts. The subsequent sections highlight some China-specific institutions – township and village enterprises, financial systems, and the restructuring of state-owned enterprises – in light of the theory. Some general comments on the Chinese model are presented in the conclusion.

Economic development and governance: an analytical framework

There is socioeconomic interaction in any non-Robinson Crusoe world. Due to asymmetric information and differences in individual preferences, many socioeconomic transactions need some governance structure: that is, contracts or institutional arrangements. From the perspective of enforcement, the contract structures governing social activities fall into two categories. (1) A relational contract is defined as a self-enforcing contract form involving long-term repeated games between fixed players. Their interactions are usually limited in certain areas and in the long run, relevant information to the parties is observable but unverifiable and hence unenforceable by a third party, such as a court or arbitrator. This kind of self-enforcing contract is also called an implicit contract or an informal institution. (2) A formal contract refers to a contract that can be verified and enforced by the court or arbitrators. Considering the fact that the court or arbitrators have less information than is held by the involved parties, formal contracts have a more demanding information structure than relational contracts. A formal contract is also referred to as an explicit contract or a formal institution.

These two different contractual forms apply to different areas. Because of asymmetric information or unverifiability by a third party, for one-off and finite horizon games, we know from the familiar backward induction approach in game theory that inefficiencies may occur. If an infinitely repeated game relationship is formed by introducing a relational contract arrangement, Pareto improvement equilibrium can be sustained as long as the discount rate is sufficiently high (in other words, if the parties are patient enough). The enforcement of a formal contract requires that the parties involved have rational expectations about future events and can specify benefit and cost allocation in all contingencies. Moreover, the information structure also requires the content and enforcement of the contract to be verified by the court or arbitrator at a low cost. Thus, the enforcement of formal contracts is more demanding than that of implicit contracts, especially in developing and transition economies like China. Generally speaking, the set of feasible implicit contracts is much greater than that of explicit contracts. Basu (2001) presented a "core theorem"[1] showing that any transaction that can be enforced by formal contract can also be enforced by relational contract.

The traditional theoretical research on relational contracts focuses on single markets.[2] Wang (2005, 2006) extends the single-market relational contract to interlinked relational contracts. This new framework can analyze the interactions between the degree of division of labor and governance structure. Put simply, efficient governance structure is a function of the market's extent and degree of specialization. In early stages of development, markets are either missing or imperfect, and interlinked contracts are an efficient alternative. Development itself will unravel the contractual interlinkage along the way.

A typical case is the contractual relationship between a landlord and tenant in an agrarian society. The tenant usually pays his rent in kind as agreed upon, which interacts on product and land markets. As a form of risk sharing, the landlord and tenant may also use a sharecropping arrangement to share risks, interacting on insurance markets. Furthermore, the landlord may even offer loans to the tenant, and they would interact once again in the credit market. Thus, the same pair of parties interacts in multiple markets simultaneously.[3] These interlinked contracts can thus make up for the lack of or flaws in specialized markets and achieve Pareto improvements. The kind of contract is particularly relevant in developing economies where market failure or market imperfection is ubiquitous.[4]

In rural areas of transitional China, we can also observe the phenomenon of interlinked contracts. For example, family A may ask family B to lend a hand in building houses without financial payment. When harvesting time arrives, family B may collect on this favor by asking family A for assistance. This arrangement can effectively address the issue of a missing labor market for rural construction and harvesting. The advantage of interlinked contracts lies in alleviating the problem of moral hazard and adverse selection that may exist in a single market by offsetting losses in one market with gains in another. Put differently, interlinked contracts internalize the externalities across the markets. Therefore, interlinked contracts can enlarge the feasible set of relational contracts; unviable transactions in a single market may become viable with interlinked contracts since people care more about the net surplus in the bundled transactions. The social structure supported by interlinked contracts is contextual and often very complex.

To sum up, appropriate governance depends on the degree of division of labor and the extent of markets. In less developed regions with missing or imperfect markets, interlinked contracts can function in place of an effective governance structure, substituting for missing markets or internalizing externalities across markets.[5] Across varied stages of economic development and in different countries, economic contracts always show some degree of relationship and interlinkage. In fact, both interlinked relational contracts and formal contracts are basically social games, so there is always a need to achieve equilibrium. Relational contracts self-enforce through long-term repeated games. According to the well-known folk theorem in game theory, an infinitely repeated game may have multiple equilibria. Therefore players may have different expectations as to the equilibrium outcome, making coordination costly in the absence of relational contracts. In addition, contractual interlinkage actually enlarges the set of feasible contracts.

In the case of multiple equilibria, there are several social mechanisms to coordinate on some efficient equilibrium. One of the mechanisms is through "focal points" (like conventions, traditions and social norms). Historically, the set of social norms expressed by Confucianism acted as a means to choose some efficient equilibrium in Chinese agrarian society, where numerous socioeconomic interactions were sustained by interlinked relational contracts. Another mechanism is through authority. Unlike the focal point mechanism, which relies on agents' shared beliefs, the mechanism of authority is expressed by some third party who acts as a coordinator; effective governments may function in this role. Interestingly, governments may also coordinate economic activities indirectly through ideologies, which then function as social norms or focal points.

Interlinked and relational contracts can promote economic development when markets are either missing or imperfect. However, ironically, development itself may well destroy the contractual structure through the following two mechanisms. (1) With economic development, markets become more specialized and broader in scope, while the division of labor increases. This may cause the contractual interlinkage among the fixed parties to unravel. In the aforementioned example, when specialized markets are developed, the interlinked contracts between landlord and tenant may be reduced to separate transactions on specialized markets. (2) Thicker arm's length markets, involving a broader segment of the population, reduce the search cost for a potential trading partner, while also undermining the relative advantages of relational contracts.

The comparative advantages of relational versus formal contracts may also be viewed from the perspective of enforcement. Since relational contracts are self-enforcing, they incur almost no cost of enforcement by the third party. The introduction of formal institutions, such as courts and a professional police force, will usually incur large set-up costs; when the market size is limited, this is not cost-effective. Hence, interlinked and relational contracts are cost-effective during the early stages of development. With increased economic development, extended market size requires that transactions go beyond fixed parties to enable scale economies, and even though relational contracts may not be a hindrance to effective transactions, formal contracts become more cost-effective. In other words, the relational contract incurs no fixed costs but faces increasing marginal costs as the market expands, while the formal contract incurs fixed costs, but faces diminishing marginal costs as the market grows.

China's economic miracle in transitioning from a planned economy to a market economy can be better understood within this framework. In essence, the transition is a process of more complete markets replacing missing or imperfect markets. As stated earlier, a good match between the development of markets and governance structure is crucial for good economic performance. Chinese-style gradualism exploits the original interlinked and relational governance structure until formal alternatives are available, in stark contrast with the Russian-style radicalism which dismantled the original governance structure almost overnight, yet failed to replace it with a more formal alternative.

In the case of China, original governance systems remained in place for a long time after the transition process had begun in both rural and urban sectors. In the rural sector, because of the low labor mobility sustained by *hukou*, a rigid residency permit system, interlinked relationships across credit, labor, and product markets were not dismantled. In the urban sector, the dismantling of the original governance structures in the state sector was gradual. During the process, people interacted with their work units (*danwei*) on interlinked markets for health care, education and housing. These interactions made up for imperfect and missing markets during the early transition period.

In the next sections we look in detail at how various forms of interlinked institutions contributed to the Chinese miracle, by highlighting the cases of township and village enterprises (TVEs) the reform of financial sector and the reform of SOEs. It will be shown that interlinked institutions played a pivotal role and that sequencing matters a lot for transition.

The township and village enterprise as an interlinked contract

The township and village enterprise (TVE) is a unique economic organization in the process of China's transition, which is not seen in other transition and developing economies. However, it was *a priori* not clear that TVEs would emerge and prosper in China.[6] In fact, the phenomenon of the TVE is at odds with the conventional wisdom that state ownership or mixed ownership is inefficient.

Table 5.1 shows the importance of 1984 in the development of TVEs; it is since then that joint-stock companies and private firms have really emerged and thrived.[7] By comparing statistics between 1983 and 1984, we also know that the previous rural community enterprises did not become the main body of TVEs. Rather, most of the TVEs were newly created firms. Township government-sponsored firms or village government-sponsored firms are collective firms, while others are non-collective firms.

Collective TVEs were usually on a large scale, and the study of production efficiency at collective TVEs has shown little difference from that of non-collective ones (Svejnar 1990; Pitt and Putterman 1992). Until the early 1990s,

Table 5.1 China's TVEs, 1983–88

Year	Total	Township collectives	Village collectives	Partnerships	Private
1983	134.64	33.81	100.83	0	0
1984	606.52	40.15	146.15	90.63	329.59
1985	1222.45	41.95	143.04	112.11	925.35
1986	1515.31	42.55	130.22	109.34	1233.20
1987	1750.10	42.01	116.27	118.75	1473.07
1988	1888.17	42.45	116.65	119.99	1609.18

Note: Unit = 10,000.
Source: Hu and Zheng (1996).

collective TVEs accounted for the majority of TVE production. In their early 1990s heyday, TVEs accounted for 27 percent of industrial output and nearly two-thirds of the non-state sector in industrial output, while the private sector accounted for only 15 percent of industrial output. Since the property rights of collective TVEs were not clearly defined, the efficiency and productivity of collective TVEs challenges the conventional wisdom on the role of clear-cut property rights, which usually claims that well-defined property rights are a prerequisite for economic growth. This has kindled heated debates among economists and other social scientists. Weitzman and Xu (1993), among others, argue that the efficiency of collective TVEs (i.e. community-based enterprises) may be attributed to a cooperative relationship sustained by a repeated game among related parties. However, this theory cannot explain the decline of TVEs after the mid-1990s.

The theory of interlinked relational contracts accounts for both the emergence and the decline of TVEs. To understand the efficiency significance of this arrangement of control and earnings rights, it is necessary to view it from the perspective of interlinked relational contracts. Due to low labor mobility and missing markets in the early stages of reform, community residents and local governments (more precisely, government officials) developed long-term relationships and multi-market interlinkages. For example, local governments not only directly purchased farm produce from rural residents, they also provided public infrastructure like education and irrigation works, while community residents paid taxes and fees to local governments and their agents. This relationship was not governed by formal institutions, but was based on self-enforcing interlinked relational contracts. Since both parties have incentives to expand production, because the government will gain revenue and the community residents will gain income, this cooperative arrangement is Pareto efficient. In addition, because of these common interests, the government was less likely to appropriate profits from entrepreneurs. In the absence of well-developed formal markets, a strong relationship between the government and entrepreneurs becomes even more crucial, as entrepreneurs count on the government to get subsidies and access to credit, land, labor and public goods. Second, due to rigid constraints on labor mobility, community residents formed interlinked relational contracts. This kind of relationship was also formed among the members, who interacted with each other across several markets. Collective TVEs acted as a nexus for creating relationships between entrepreneurs, communities, community residents and local governments. This kind of institutional arrangement generated a large economic surplus, which was shared among the parties.

Figure 5.1 examines the interlinked relational contracts in rural sectors, focusing on the transactions between the local community, TVEs and the community government in more detail. Based on the work of Byrd and Gelb (1990), it highlights the financial flows between these stakeholders, and demonstrates how the TVE can be seen as an interlinked institutional arrangement.

Because of the limited amount of initial accumulated public funds, the lion's share of funding of TVEs came from within the community, financed by community residents or by loans from credit unions and banks. Furthermore, a substantial part of raw material, land and labor, was coordinated and allocated by town or village authorities. To enjoy these favorable arrangements by governments, TVEs had to meet the profit target set by the government and pay the corresponding share of profit to the government, share control rights with the government, and accept government-appointed managers.

As documented by Byrd and Gelb (1990), Figure 5.1 shows financial flows among township enterprises and township and county institutions. Township enterprises paid direct and indirect taxes to the township tax collector and paid management fees to their supervisory agency, the township industrial corporation (TIC). The after-tax profit was shared between the TIC and the firms. Remitted township enterprise profits flow upwards through the system, as an important source of funding for township government salaries and overheads as well as for discretionary spending. Salaries and benefits of township governmental officials come from three main sources: budgetary allocation for salaries, profits remitted from township enterprise and the shared proportion of above-quota tax revenue. Figure 5.1 also shows the interactions among the firms, banks and the community. In particular, the individuals deposit their savings in the banks, which in turn lend to the firms. Thus, it would be more instructive to take TVEs as a kind of transitional governance structure to internalize externalities and generate social surplus through interlinked relationships.

Interlinked relational contracts also explain why TVEs were transformed into private firms after the mid-1990s.[8] As specialized product, credit and labor markets developed more, and property rights became more secure in the mid-1990s, TVEs as interlinked contracts were gradually dismantled.

Reform in the financial sector reconsidered

The process of transition of financial institutional arrangements is very enlightening, in both formal and informal interlinked institutions.

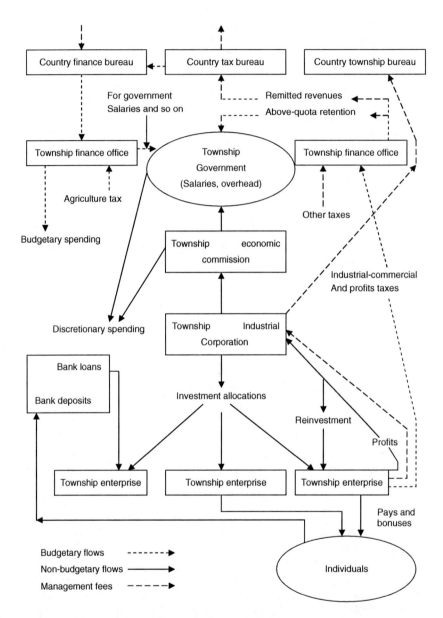

Figure 5.1 Financial flow among stakeholders in TVEs.
Source: *China's Private Sector* (1989).

From 1978 to 1995, the major sources of credit were the Agricultural Bank of China and rural credit unions. The Agricultural Bank of China reopened in 1979 and expanded its branches into counties. These branches were in charge of supervising rural credit unions. A rural credit union is a collective financial institution aimed at providing working capital for agricultural production. In the 1980s, rural credit unions played a crucial role in financing rural growth. The Agricultural Bank of China was first established as a policy bank to support agricultural development, but it was not long before it became commercialized and departed from its intended purpose, making commercial loans instead of policy-related loans.

However, with the economic transition deepening and labor mobility increasing, the interlinked relationships between the community and rural credit unions were weakened. Due to the government's inappropriate intervention, the functions performed by rural credit unions were weakened and even became harmful. Statistics show that the loan deposit ratio of rural credit unions was 0.41 in 1984, 0.28 in 1990, and only 0.19 in 1996, which means that there was actually fund capital flowing out from rural areas.[9]

Fortunately, during this period there were various forms of informal finance, such as rural cooperative foundations, private money houses, and rotating credit associations.[10] They provided important support for agricultural production and for the development of TVEs. Table 5.2 shows the sources of financing for start-up private enterprises based on a survey from 1988.

As shown in Table 5.2, private firms' initial financing channels were very limited. Internal financing, including personal savings and borrowing from friends and relatives, was dominant (52 percent) and supplemented by the fund pool of employees. Loans from banks and credit unions also comprised quite a large share (41.1 percent), which can be explained by the various paths to these loans demonstrated in Table 5.3.

As shown in Table 5.3, private firms' access to financial institutions was greatly facilitated by the personal guarantee of village heads; other personal connections were also significant. This kind of political and social collateral is an effective mechanism to overcome market imperfections.

The second stage of development started in 1996, when rural credit unions were totally separated from the Agricultural Bank of China. A formal financial institution system comprising this bank, rural credit unions and the agricultural development bank was formed in rural areas. The focus of rural financial

Table 5.2 Sources of start-up capital of the sample private firms (%)

Own capital	Loans from banks and credit cooperatives	Loans from relatives and friends	Workers' contribution (gongren daizi)	Other sources
37	41.1	15	1.9	5

Source: *China's Private Sector* (1989).

Table 5.3 Access to banks and credit cooperatives (%)

Using collective property as collateral (via village head)	Banks and cooperatives think them promising	Personal connections with staff in banks credit cooperatives	Using own property as collateral
32	30	8	30

Source: *China's Private Sector* (1989).

system reform now shifted to the reform of rural credit unions. Farmers, businessmen and various economic organizations were invited to hold shares of credit unions, community financial organizations serving farmers, agriculture, and rural economic development. Although there still appeared to be complete formal financial organizations in rural areas and credit unions still performed important functions, in reality credit unions were steadily losing importance. In 1999, 2000, 2001 and 2002, the ratio of the loan balance of rural sectors to total loans was 10.69, 10, 10.8 and 10.4 percent respectively. In contrast, state-owned commercial banks drew as much as RMB 300 billion from rural areas in the form of deposits in 2001. For Postal Saving banks, deposits were approximately RMB 600 billion, while deposits may have been even larger for credit unions.[11] Most small and medium-sized private firms still had to rely on informal finance. However, with market expansion and the weakening of interlinked relationships between economic agents, the cost for financing based on interlinked relational contracts increased greatly. This was marked by ever-increasing interest rates in the informal financial sectors and greater force used in the enforcement of contracts. Due to these changes, the government attempted to suppress and regulate informal finance, although the effectiveness of this policy to fix the problem was doubtful.

As demonstrated, there were two stages during which the formal financial system successfully performed its functions in the transition of China's rural sectors. From the 1980s to the early 1990s, formal interlinked arrangements among community members, the community government and formal financial institutions were productive, becoming less productive in the late 1990s with the expanding of markets. In contrast, from the early 1990s the self-enforcing informal financial system based on interlinked relationship contracts became relatively more important, showing that in the process of transition, original formal contracts were dismantled while informal financial systems stepped in as a viable alternative.

However, formal finance was not necessarily inefficient. Inefficiency involves both standards of appraisal and approaches of appraisal. Conventional efficiency standards only apply to a single market or sector and neglect the efficiency implications of interlinked arrangements. In a perfect market economy, this approach to assessing the efficiency of institutional arrangements is valid because specialized markets are very common and the efficiency of transactions can be examined on the basis of a single market. However, in transitional economies like China, some markets either do not exist, or are imperfect. In this case, the examination of the efficiency of institutional arrangements should consider the case of interlinking markets. For financial systems, long-term relationships require examination of the long-term effects of institutional arrangements, while the interlinking of markets requires an investigation of the externality of institutional arrangements among markets and sectors.

Since state-owned commercial banks, which dominated formal financial institutions in China, had a clear purpose of serving (large) SOEs, the examination of their efficiency should focus on how well they supported the reform of SOEs. Public ownership was dominant in cities for a long time. The inefficiency of urban sectors and barely sustainable social governance were great challenges to this transition. The state tried different transitional means to incentivize the SOE managers, such as giving more control and cash flow (*fangquan rangli*) to the managers, and implementing enterprise contracting (*qiye chengbaozhi*) after the mid-1990s, before large-scale privatization.

These transitional means were supported by corresponding fiscal and financial arrangements and restructuring among SOEs, to reduce the social costs of transition. There are at least three forms of subsidies to SOEs. The first is loans with low interest rates and outstanding debt. According to statistics of the World Bank, financing from this channel accounted for 1.72 percent of GDP each year from 1985 to 1994, with 1992 the highest at 3.6 percent. The second form is subsidies transferred from state banks. The third is large amounts of non-performing loans (NPLs) which SOEs owe the state banks. These loans are unlikely to be repaid and can be taken as a kind of implicit subsidy to the enterprises. It is estimated that during the period 1985 to 1996, on average the bad debt of China's SOEs accounted for 9.7 percent of GDP, with 1993 the highest at 18.81 percent. Based on a survey by Zhou Xiaochuan in 2004,[12] the sources of NPLs are shown in Table 5.4.

It is evident that 80 percent of the NPLs can be attributed to the cost of gradualism. According to the calculation by Chen and Zhuo (2006), the costs borne by state banks are as high as 23979.38 billion *yuan*.

This is not the whole story. To corporatize the loss-making state banks, the government worked out a comprehensive package to spin off the NPLs. As shown in Figure 5.2, the package is an umbrella arrangement to address the

Table 5.4 The making of non-performing loans (%)

Inappropriate interventions by central and local governments	Cheap credit to SOEs	Poor legal enforcement	Restructuring of SOEs by government	Mismanagement by banks
30	30	10	10	20

Source: Chen and Zhuo (2006).

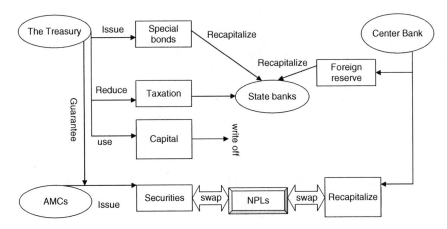

Figure 5.2 The comprehensive package for non-performing loans.
Source: Based on Chen and Zhuo (2006).

problems facing banks and SOEs. The ministry of finance recapitalized the state banks using both special treasury bonds and foreign reserves. At the same time, asset management companies were there to make the debt-equity swap by securitization of the NPLs. The efficiency of the interlinked arrangement can be justified on the ground that the seemingly low efficiency of state banks actually relaxed the constraints facing the SOEs reform.

The reform in the financial sector shows how interlinked institutional arrangements worked, in both informal and formal finance. These arrangements were an effective substitute for missing credit markets in the rural and urban sectors. In particular, the arrangement in the formal financial sector (i.e. the state banking sector) should not be examined alone, since it relaxed the financial constraints and laid the foundation for more subtle reforms of the SOE sector.

Reform of state-owned enterprises reconsidered

The reform of SOEs constitutes another case in point of interlinked arrangements as a transitional institution. During the old days of the planned economy, there were no specialized markets and SOEs used to provide a whole range of services to their employees, like housing and health care, which would otherwise have been provided in markets. SOEs covered so large a part of people's socioeconomic life that it is easy to imagine the difficulties in dismantling the system in a radical way. In this regard, the state took a gradualist approach to the reform and various interlinked institutional arrangements, as effective substitutes for missing and imperfect markets were carried out.

Managers, the government, employees and banks were the four major player-stakeholders in the reform of SOEs. Restructuring the SOEs involved dismantling the highly interlinked arrangements among the four parties of the planning era.

Compared with the quick privatization in Russia, the Chinese style of SOE restructuring was characterized by gradual dismantling of the interlinkage, with concurrent development of the relevant markets.

There are several ways to do this. One of the arrangements is subsidization of losses of SOEs by fiscal revenue. At the beginning, subsidies take the form of subsidy for loss and price subsidy (for instance, an SOE can get inputs from other SOEs at a price lower than the market price). Explicit subsidies to SOEs from 1985 to 1994 by the state budget amounted to 5.63 percent of GDP (Zhang 1998). In 2000 the price subsidy alone was as much as 104.228 billion *yuan*. In 2003 social relief expenditure amounted to RMB 21.769 billion *yuan*. A large part of subsidies came from taxation of the agricultural sector, TVEs and private enterprises. As the reform of decentralization proceeded, the revenue of the central government decreased and so did financial subsidies, from 7.5 percent of GDP in 1985 to 2.2 percent of GDP in 1994. To compensate for the declining fiscal subsidies, loans from formal financial institutions like commercial banks came onto the stage to finance the restructuring of SOEs. According to 1996 World Bank estimates, from 1987 to 1995, loans from the banking system by the government and SOEs accounted for 9 percent of GDP, of which the lion's share of 8.6 percent went to SOEs.

Along with subsidies from fiscal revenue and the state financial sector, there were also various subtle transitional labor contractual arrangements between the state and employees, leading to towards a full dismantling of SOEs after the mid-1990s. Among these institutions, *xiagang* is a very telling feature of the interlinked arrangement.

Xiagang describes a system whereby SOE workers who have been laid off due to the poor performance of the enterprises still maintain some nominal relationship with their enterprises; these employees receive a "subsistence level of salary" or other kinds of benefits (such as housing or health care) from their enterprises. *Xiagang* can be taken as a substitute for the lack of an insurance market or social security system.

As evidenced in a survey by the Development Research Center of the State Council (2005), which elaborated on 46 kinds of specific costs of SOE restructuring, the main costs included severance pay, payment for the arrears of delayed wages, welfare payments and payment for social security. Per capita payments of central government controlled SOEs amounted to 14,000 *yuan*, while per capita payments of local government controlled SOEs amounted to 40,500 *yuan*. The payments were mostly made out of firms' net assets. In the survey, 44 percent of firms had to resort to rent from controlled land ownership to make welfare payments, since their net assets were less than aggregate welfare payments, and one out of five firms needed finance from their holding companies to make the payments.

The survey also documents the conditional acquisition of loss-making SOEs by other firms. The acquiring firms had to commit to keep the original employees from the acquired firms. This affected 45 percent of central government controlled SOEs and 60 percent of local government controlled SOEs.

The SOE sector used to be the commanding height of China's urban economy in the era of the planned economy. A *danwei* was not just a workplace; it was a social and political organization since all markets are suppressed, where different resources were exchanged between the workers and the state. The workers provided labor and the state reciprocated with wage, housing, health care and a collection of other goods and services that otherwise would be provided through markets. In this regard, the *danwei* system itself is a highly interlinked relational contract and the nature of the reform of the urban sector is the dismantling of the interlinked arrangement and replacing it with specialized markets (goods, labor, credit, housing, health care, schooling, etc.). As highlighted in the case of *xiagang* above, due to undeveloped markets of labor and other goods and services, for a long time during the transition the government still used various kinds of interlinked arrangements. Only after the mid-1990s, when the specialized markets were more developed, and most SOE reform was privatized, did there begin to be massive lay-offs.

Concluding remarks

This chapter presents a theory of interlinked relational contracts to account for the miracle of Chinese gradualist reform. There are two important dimensions of the transition from a central planned economy to a market economy. On the one hand, the transition is a process of dismantling the planning system and the creation of specialized markets. At the beginning of the process, markets are either missing or highly imperfect. On the other hand, the missing and imperfect markets during the dismantling of the old system need some alternative governance which is neither market nor planning, but something in between.

Interlinked arrangements are a kind of transitional governance, which took various forms during China's transition. Several cases have been examined: TVEs, reform of financial sector and reform of SOEs. It has been shown that the sequencing of reforms matters a lot. China's reform started from the rural sector and then moved on to the urban sector. This is sequentially optimal since the urban sector was harder to dismantle due to its highly organized system, whereas the rural sector's informal mechanisms (social capital) for finance and risk sharing led to the TVE boom. The success of rural reforms greatly relaxed the constraints facing urban reform and the growth of TVEs and other private firms more than made up for the declining output share of state firms. Even within the urban sector, the sequencing of reforms also played an important role, depending on the degree of completeness and perfection of various markets.

China's experience is at odds with the so-called "Washington Consensus", an argument based on complete markets and clear-cut property rights. As a prescription for transition economies and developing economies, it is misleading since the markets during transition are definitely incomplete, and as the Chinese case shows, where there are incomplete markets, interlinked arrangements may be the best feasible choice. Interlinked arrangements imply that property rights are rather ambiguous, as in the case of TVEs. Interestingly, from the perspective of the enforcement of contracts, formal contracts are likely to be imperfect and the interlinked contract can overcome this problem to some extent, since interlinked contracts can internalize externalities of otherwise separate markets.

As was noted at the beginning, interlinked contracts are an effective governance structure when markets are either missing or imperfect. When markets are more complete and perfect, it should give way to alternative governance structures. In particular, the boundary between the government and the market should be more clear-cut. Otherwise, further economic development may be undermined. Many authors have pointed out that crony capitalism was partly responsible for the East Asian crises in late 1990s.[13] As the interlinked arrangements unravel, profound socioeconomic and political changes may occur.[14] In this sense, China still has a long way to go towards a full modernization.

6 The East Asian Development Model reconsidered with implications for China

After World War II, four Asian newly industrialized economies (NIEs) – Hong Kong, Taiwan, Singapore and Korea – stand out as new members of the club of developed economies.[1] This has drawn much interest in the East Asian Development Model (EADM) and its implications for economic theories of development. There is myriad literature discussing the EADM. In particular, the World Bank published *The East Asian Miracle: Economic Growth and Public Policy* in 1993, to draw general lessons from the East Asian development experience that could be applied to other developing countries. The World Bank emphasizes the following four points. (1) Macroeconomic management is important in that stable commercial environments and low inflation rates are conducive to investment. Prudential fiscal policy accompanied by inclusive economic growth is also a plus. (2) Strong government management enables fast growth of output and employment through interactions between industrial sectors and government. (3) Industrialization with active state intervention supports policies that promote the export of industrial products. (4) The government clearly stated the conditions on which firms could enjoy favorable policies and credibly threatened to withdraw support if these conditions were not satisfied.[2] In the early twenty-first century, the EADM attracted much academic attention again. A case in point is *Rethinking the East Asian Miracle*, a volume edited by Stiglitz and Yusuf (2001), also produced by the World Bank. The book reflects upon the EADM in a historical perspective. More specifically and much earlier on, there are trade-based theories to explain the EADM, such as the Flying Goose model by Akamatsu (1962), among others.[3]

The above studies almost all conduct macro analysis of the EADM, which characterizes its aggregate features, but is inadequate as a theoretical explanation because it does not delve into the microeconomic and the institutional foundations of these economies. A volume edited by Aoki, Kim and Okuno-Fujiwara (1997) touches upon government's role of enhancing the market system in the development of East Asia. It also discusses how institutional arrangements address issues such as coordination failure of technology adoption and financial systems. However, again its take on the EADM is static. It does not develop a stage theory identifying optimal institutional arrangements corresponding to different stages of economic development. It can partly explain the success of the EADM at early stages, but cannot account for its later transition and relative stagnation. Hence its policy implications for developing economies are not robust.

Theoretically speaking, the first question we should ask is, is there an EADM? If there is, what are the defining features of this model? The answer is affirmative for the former question; although East Asian countries differ in polity and economy, they have much in common. These commonalities form the subject of the EADM. From the perspective of development patterns and institutions, East Asian economies share at least the following five characteristics. (1) During economic take-off after World War II, authoritarian governments played a pivotal role in economic development by adopting extensive industrial policies to intervene in the economy. (2) The rule of law was not as pervasive as in the Western world, while social norms based on long-term relationships played an important role in socioeconomic life. (3) The economic structure was centralized and there were a few big firms and banks as major players in the economic arena. Banks had long-term relationships with firms and provided the dominant source of financing for large corporations. (4) Economic success at preliminary stages, once dubbed as Asia's miracle, was followed by economic crises in many economies at the end of 1990s. Japan, for instance, began stagnating even in the early 1990s. (5) From the perspective of political transformation, the free market system was accompanied by a political democratization process in these economies after 30 years of rapid growth. Interestingly, China's development since reform and opening up shares the first three characteristics of the EADM, but not the latter two. Since China is similar to East Asian economies in social structure and culture, the EADM is significant to China's transition.

One study closely related to our perspective is Li (2003), which presents a framework for examining the EADM. Li identifies two contractual forms of governance: relationship-based governance and rule-based governance. The former is enforced by long-term repeated games between fixed agents and the latter is enforced by a third party (a court, for example). Relation-based governance is self-enforcing in the sense that it does not need a third party to enforce it. Rule-based governance requires relevant contract information to be enforced by a third party and entails high set-up costs associated with investment in institutional infrastructure.[4] So these two governance structures have their own comparative advantages. At the early stages of economic development when market size is small, relational contracts are a better governance structure in that they place minimal demands on the contract information structure (no need for verification by a third party), which makes it possible to implement a larger contract set. Moreover, it also reduces the cost of contracting since it saves on the cost of establishing and maintaining a legal system. But with economic development and corresponding expansion of the market, relationship-based contracts become less effective because their marginal cost increases as more parties become involved in each transaction. In contrast, under rule-based governance the marginal cost incurred when parties are added to a transaction is decreasing. In other words, rule-based governance exhibits an institutional scale economy, characterized by a large fixed cost associated with maintaining institutional infrastructure. Interestingly, this framework explains not only the success of the EADM, but also the emergence of the East Asian crisis: during the early stages of East Asian development, relationship-based governance played an important role in the absence of formal institutions. With economic development and market expansion, this governance structure gradually gave way to rule-based governance, but it may be associated with some unstable dynamics during the transition period, which can lead to crises.

The framework presented by Li (2003) is insightful. A drawback of his analysis is that without formal models the interaction between market extent and institutional change remains a black box. It is not clear how a relationship-based society is transformed to a rule-based society. We need to characterize the micro-mechanism underlying institutional change caused by expansion of market extent. We will characterize the relationship between the degree of division of labor and institutions in light of the theory of interlinked and relational contracts (Braverman and Stiglitz 1982; Wang 2007). In essence, the theory is about the relationship between economic development and contract form. The basic idea is that effective contract form (institution) is a function of the extent of the market. In a developing economy with a limited market extent and division of labor, agents engage in multiple types of interlinked transactions. A typical case is share tenancy in agriculture. In a developing economy, landlords and tenants make transactions not only on the product market (tenants may buy agricultural produce from landlords), but also interact on labor market (the landlord employs the tenant), credit market (the landlords provides loans to the tenant), and insurance market (for instance, through sharecropping arrangements). In an economy with more complete markets, economic transactions occur on different specialized markets among anonymous traders. Contracts which are unprofitable at arm's length may be viable in interlinked transactions. That is, interlinked markets expand the feasible set of viable relational contracts. During economic development, interlinked markets are replaced by specialized markets and interlinked and relational contracts are replaced by rule-based contracts. This matching between market size and institutions is key to understanding economic development.

Based on the above theory a "stage theory" can be developed that argues that government should play different roles at different stages of development. The basic idea is that the degree of market completeness differs across developmental stages, and accordingly that the appropriate degree of government intervention also varies across stages. A political system and set of policies that proved successful at one stage may become an obstacle to development during a later stage. This theory is also a theory of the political economy of development. We will characterize the relationship between the degree of market completeness and optimal political system and policy as well as interaction between government and entrepreneurs (and/or other social groups).

The contributions of this new theoretical framework are as follows. (1) It explains why institutions are endogenous in economic development. At early stages of economic development, with low division of labor and hence incomplete markets, self-enforcing interlinked and relational contracts sustain socioeconomic functioning. (2) From the perspective of public policy and the relationship between government and market, governments with autonomy and capacity can coordinate economic activities and promote economic development by interlinking relationships between economic agents to make up for missing markets. (3) With economic development, the division of labor increases and the interlinking of markets gradually unravels. To sustain socioeconomic functioning, formal contracts (democratic and legal systems) now play increasingly important roles. Therefore, the timing of transition to a formal legal system is key to further development and modernization.

This chapter is organized as follows. The next section discusses how governments with high autonomy and state capacity can use interlinked relationship-based institutional arrangements to make up for missing markets and foster economic development. There is a further analysis of the relationship between law, social norms and economic development. Then we look at how institutions based on interlinking relationships were transformed through the course of East Asian development. This is followed by a discussion of the general implications of the EADM for economic development and institutional change from the perspective of comparative economic development. Finally some implications of the EADM for China's economic transition are described.

State and economic development: industrial policies as an interlinked relational contract

Background of industrial policies

The role industrial that policies played in East Asian economic development has attracted much research interest in political science and sociology (Johnson 1982; Amsden 1989; Wade 1990; Evans 1995).[5] A wider definition of industrial policy is adopted here that includes all structural policies aimed at making up for missing or imperfect markets. These structural policies usually achieve desirable social goals by changing relative prices of products or factors.

Interest in industrial policy research has been rekindled in mainstream economics in recent years. Over the past 30 years international organizations like the World Bank and the IMF promoted free market policy (the so-called "Washington Consensus") in the developing world, but this yielded economic stagnation. On the other, planned economies like the former USSR experienced economic failure in the second half of twentieth century, which shows that government intervention in all economic activities is not appropriate. The practice of East Asian economies lies somewhere in between. Historically, industrialized countries or regions (Japan and the four Asian NIEs, especially South Korea) in East Asia all implemented active industrial policies that have the following characteristics. (1) Protectionist trade policy and exchange policy was used to support large industrial companies. (2) Pillar industries with strong backward linkages or forward linkages were encouraged. (3) Banks provided not only long-term financing to firms, but also explicit or implicit subsidies. (4) Governments helped to promote markets for the products of large conglomerates (*chaebols* in Korea and *keiretsus* in Japan, for example). These distorting industrial policies of "getting prices wrong" facilitated economic catch-up in these East Asian economies (Johnson 1982; Amsden 1989; Wade 1990). Nowadays both academicians and policy-makers take a more realistic view of the relationship between the government and the market. The relevant problem is not *whether* government should intervene, but *how*. In particular, in recent decades, globalization has posed a great challenge for national and international economic structures. It is essential to study the role of industrial policies in the shadow of globalization.

Special economic structure of developing countries

Although industrial policies are important in practice, theories concerning industrial policies seem rather undeveloped. Only in the last ten years has a consensus on the "Washington Consensus" been reached: economic policies adopted in developed market economies don't work in developing countries. This is because the economic structure of developing countries is different from that of developed countries and thus calls for different economic policies. As the economic historian Gerschenkron (1962) pointed out long ago:

> In a number of important historical instances, industrialization processes, when launched at length in a backward country, showed considerable differences with more advanced countries, not only with regard to the speed of development (the rate of industrial growth) but also with regards to the productive and organizational structures of industry ... these differences in the speed and character of industrial development were to a considerable extent the result of application of institutional instruments for which there was little or no counterpart in an established industrial country.

In terms of economic structure, there are two salient features unique to developing economies. (1) Compared with the complete market system in developed countries, markets are either missing or imperfect in developing countries. (2) Developing countries are far from the world technological possibility frontier.

These two differences are essential to the understanding of economic development and governments' role in economic development. Missing markets imply that there is room for Pareto improving interventions; being far from the world technology possibility frontier implies that developing countries can learn or simply mimic existing technologies without undertaking their own research and development. Therefore, appropriate government intervention can improve resource allocation by facilitating technology adoption. In particular, as is elaborated later, in the absence of well-functioning markets, governments can make Pareto improving interventions through interlinked institutional arrangements. Such interventions can promote the use of existing technologies, mobilize resources and investment, and help ensure a stable relationship among key economic players. In terms used by Acemoglu, Aghion and Zilibotti (2006), this stage of development is investment-based growth, in contrast to the innovation-based stage where the technology is on the world frontier and hence innovation is the key to growth, as has happened in developed economies. In the investment-based development stage, industrial policies establish contractual relationships between politicians and firms, which form the basis for long-horizon investments.

Some necessary conditions for success of industrial policies

At the stage of investment-based growth, the key issue is how to effectively mobilize and organize resources in the economy. At this stage, due to missing or imperfect markets, resource allocation through the market is generally not Pareto efficient. Appropriate government intervention can improve resource allocation (Greenwald and Stiglitz 1986). Theoretically, governments can improve resource allocation and achieve Pareto improvement through appropriate industrial policies, but these are not easy to implement. There are at least the following necessary conditions for the government to improve resource allocation. (1) The government's objective is to maximize social welfare with different social groups being assigned relatively equal weights. In other words, the government should have high autonomy; that is, they should not be prone to capture by interest groups. An egalitarian society is more likely to satisfy this condition. (2) The government should have enough state capacity and sufficient policy instruments to intervene in the economy. (3) The form and extent of intervention are contingent on the development stage. Therefore, when the market system has fully developed, the role of government should change accordingly.

Economic development via the EADM satisfies the above three conditions. First, after World War II, for most governments using the EADM, economic development was one of the most important ways to achieve political legitimacy. Shortly after the war, the governments of Japan, South Korea and Taiwan all lacked political legitimacy. Japan had just been defeated in 1945; South Korea had just gained independence from Japanese occupation and suffered great economic loss during the Korean War from 1950 to 1952; the Chinese Nationalist government led by Chiang Kai-shek fled to Taiwan after it lost the Chinese civil war. Economic growth offered them political legitimacy. It is noteworthy that they all started egalitarian land reforms in the 1950s, which laid the groundwork for later inclusive economic growth. The war also played a role in shattering original elite groups and boosting social equality, which encouraged governments to pursue objectives beneficial to average citizens.

Second, authoritarian governments in East Asia have an effective bureaucratic system with effective control over economic resources and access to multiple policy instruments. Therefore they have strong state capacity. Japan's industrial policies can be traced back to the Meiji Restoration in mid-nineteenth century. The slogans of the Meiji government were "industrialization" and "Rich Nation, Strong Army". After World War II under the centralized government led by the Liberal Democratic Party (LDP), Japan's Ministry of International Trade and Industry (MITI) played a critical role in industrial policy-making and implementation (Johnson 1982). MITI had discretion to intervene in industrial development by using extensive policy instruments. The same holds true for South Korea and Taiwan. During Korea's period of rapid growth, and in particular the 1960s and 1970s, an authoritarian government led by President Park Chung-hee implemented extensive industrial policies. In Taiwan, an authoritarian national government implemented industrial policies. These governments controlled sufficient economic and financial resources necessary to implement industrial policy. It deserves attention that they are not only politically centralized, but also centralized in economic structure. A few conglomerates dominated their economies. Centralization, both political and economic, makes it easier for the government to establish long-term relationships with industry, which is helpful for implementing industrial policies.

As for the third condition, industrial policies under the EADM are stage-contingent. At the stage of economic take-off, these economies all implemented industrial policies which would be modified or abandoned later at higher level of development. For instance, Japan adopted trade liberalization policy in 1970s, which led to changes in the relationship between firms and MITI. In the 1980s, South Korea and Taiwan relied less on industrial policies and transformed the relationship between government and firms. Especially after the East Asian financial crisis in 1998, the relationship between government and firms was kept at a lower level.

How industrial policies were implemented

The theory of interlinked and relational contracts previously discussed can be used to explain industrial policies despite some differences in the specific industrial policies adopted in each EADM country. When a market is incomplete, interlinked and relational contracts can internalize externalities and make up for the missing market. To some degree, industrial policies can be taken as an interlinked and relational contract between government and firms. The relationship between government and entrepreneurs here is similar to that between a landlord and a tenant in developing countries previously discussed. This interlinked relationship, which is across multiple markets including credit, product and insurance markets, can achieve Pareto improvement. To the extent that the first necessary condition for successful industrial policies holds, industrial policies maximize social welfare. In the 1950s land market reform and special contract arrangements inside firms (lifetime employment, for example) in these economies caused firms' surpluses to be evenly distributed. Therefore, in the following analysis, we take industrial policies as maximizing the total surplus between government and firms. Missing markets at the stage of economic take-off and utilitarian government make this interlinked relationship between enterprises and government possible.

During periods of high-rate growth, governments in East Asia had several extensive policy instruments to interact with firms on multiple "markets".

First, government and firms interacted on the credit market to overcome market failure. Under the EADM, governments usually implemented credit policies through centralized financial systems dominated by banks. Laws enacted in Japan in 1949 and 1950 allowed the government to use many policy instruments to control credit markets and separated the domestic credit market from the international credit market. Japan's domestic credit market is segmented with local markets having different, government controlled interest rates. This control allowed government to pursue so-called "non-equilibrium (under equilibrium interest rate) policy". In addition, the government kept long-term loan rates and deposit rates under market equilibrium rates. This policy led to excess demand and the need for rationing, allowing the Ministry of Finance (MOF) to direct credit to large corporations with new technology (so-called "window guidance"). The credit policy of the MOF improved productivity and boosted exports. The MOF also had the authority to selectively distribute foreign exchange reserves as part of a "carrot and stick" policy to direct firms' technological choices (because firms need foreign exchange to import raw materials and new technology) (Eads and Yamamura 1987). Similar situations occurred in South Korea and Taiwan. From the 1960s to the 1990s South Korea's financial sector was mainly controlled by the government and used to implement state policy. Even in the early 1980s, most banks were still state owned and capital flow was strictly controlled. Banks were not independent market agents who maximized profits, but instead carried out government policies, promoting industrial investment, exports and growth. The government provided not only guarantees for firms' borrowing, but also state credit to banks. Government control over financial resources had a large effect on economic development. First, the government used financial control to maximize the rate of saving and capital accumulation. Second, the government allocated financial resources among industries and firms according to industrial policies in an effort to upgrade the economic structure and promote economic development. The financial sector of Taiwan remained heavily regulated by the government until the 1980s. At the economic take-off stage in Taiwan in the 1960s, the interest rate was controlled to stimulate investment and economic growth. To implement export-oriented industrial development policies, banks lent at low interest rates to favored industries. In 1980, Taiwan adopted a strategy of industrial upgrading and restructuring. Several strategic industries (such as machinery and electronics) were granted low interest rate loans from banks. It deserves attention that interactions between the government and firms on credit markets not only mitigated credit market failure, but also affected firms' technology choices through the rationing of credit.

Second, government and firms interacted on product markets to expand the market for products and allow firms to take advantage of scale economies. At the stage of economic take-off it is common practice to restrict import and encourage exports so as to augment market share of firms at home. Import quotas and high import tariffs were often used to serve this purpose. The effective rate of protection of the manufacturing sector in Japan in 1968 was above 10 percent (Noland and Pack 2003). Moreover, there were various non-tariff barriers including expensive inspection costs and rigorous product standards, which restricted competition from foreign companies. Domestic large corporations were also favored in government procurement, which helped them expand their market share at home. Therefore, enforcement of anti-trust law in Japan was very loose for domestic large corporations so as to encourage them to take advantage of economies of scale. The South Korean government also helped domestic firms to expand markets at home and abroad. Especially after President Park Chung-hee came to power in the mid-1960s, export performance was taken as the yardstick of a firm's success. To boost exports, the government reduced multiple interest rates to one single low rate and devalued the currency in 1964. The Korea Trade-Investment Promotion Agency (KOTRA) was founded by the government to conduct market research and promote export. Export companies enjoyed tax rebates when importing intermediate goods and would also be given additional rewards. Similarly, at the economic take-off stage, Taiwan's government adopted many export encouraging policies. Aside from tariff and non-tariff barriers to restrict import, the government provided subsidies and credit lines to export sectors. When there was no private investment for important projects, the government would directly establish state-owned enterprises. Under the EADM, interaction between the government and firms on domestic and international product markets helped firms enjoy economies of scale and fostered industrial growth.

Third, the government and firms interacted in insurance markets. During the early period of economic development, the technological choices of entrepreneurs were exposed to more risk because their investments were to a large degree dependent on investments in complementary sectors that were not yet in place. Also, dramatic changes in economic structure posed extra risks. Under the EADM, governments usually took many measures to share risk related to investment and technological innovation with firms. In fact, low interest rate policies and export subsidies are also a kind of insurance. Besides insurance, the government used direct subsidies to encourage R&D activities of firms. For instance, the Japanese government provided direct subsidies, low interest rate loans and preferential tax policies to support R&D and investment in high technology. In 1966, the government set up contracts for large-scale research in industrial technology to encourage enterprises to do related R&D; in the 1970s, the government gave subsidies for R&D in computer science; in the 1980s, subsidies were directed to R&D in materials, biological technology and electronic equipment (Noland and Pack 2003). In South Korea, when demand was sharply reduced, the government directed low interest rate loans to companies that were financially weak but with good fundamentals. The Taiwanese government reduced innovation costs by providing subsidies for firms' R&D activities. Interaction between government and firms on insurance markets allowed government to share the investment risk of firms. This insurance mechanism was not limited to the relationship between government and firms; the life employment system (especially in Japan) also constituted a kind of insurance for employees.

The interlinked institutional arrangements between the government and firms in the credit, product and insurance markets have already been analyzed. The interlinking implies that interaction between government and firms was based on long-term relationships. In the implementation of industrial policy, many directives of the government are unwritten or implicit, and their implementation is dependent on long-term interaction. Part of the reason why firms follow directives from government is that the relationship between government and firms is long term and multi-dimensional (Eads and Yamamura 1987). Relationships between the government and companies were similar in South Korea and Taiwan. This is exactly what we call the "interlinked and relational contract".

Since industrial policies are in essence an interlinked and relational contract between government and firms, to assure enforceability of the contract, only a limited number of large corporations can gain the government's support, and entry and exit is restricted; unrestricted entry into interlinked institutional arrangements would jeopardize the enforceability of the contract. Indeed, governments in East Asia limited the application of industrial policies to a few of the largest corporations, and therefore the whole economic structure was centralized. The interlinked institutional arrangements were not just between the government and large companies; transactions between large companies and small and medium-sized enterprises were also interlinked and relational. A large company is usually surrounded by a group of small and medium-sized firms who supply raw materials, intermediate goods and services for the large company. The large company and those small firms comprise a network of subcontracting. This interlinked relational contract is embedded in the larger contract arrangement between government and large corporations, and thus economic surplus brought about by the latter can trickle down to small and medium-sized enterprises. Because of initial egalitarian conditions and unique employment institution (say, lifetime employment), inclusive growth has been achieved.

Previously it was discussed how industrial policies, as an interlinked relational contract, address the issue of missing markets at early stages of economic development. The following is a theoretical characterization of industrial policies and their role in economic development.

First, properly implemented industrial policies address the problem of missing markets through interlinked and relational contracts. Relational contracts are in essence long-term repeated games, which usually have multiple equilibria. Differing expectations among players and interlinked contracts tend to aggravate the problem of multiple equilibria. In this case, authoritarian governments can help pick desirable equilibria by coordinating players' activities and expectations.

Second, due to missing markets, interlinked institutional arrangements distort the relative prices of factors and products. Competitive markets get prices right, while industrial policies get them wrong. At the early stages of economic development, intentionally getting the price wrong is "right" to the extent that it helps direct scarce resources to key industries and endogenously leads to the emergence and development of other industries through forward and backward linkages. Also, it can allow industries to reap economies of scale. Because firms can learn and mimic existing technologies at early stages, developing countries may achieve what Gerschenkron (1962) calls the "advantages of backwardness".

Last but not least, industrial policies are systematic institutional arrangements: transactions on the credit, product and insurance markets are interlinked. Combined with the second point just discussed, this means that the whole price system is distorted compared with that in the context of perfect competitive market. While distortion of the whole system may enhance development in early stages, it poses problems for later economic transition and liberalization. The expansion of market extent in later development calls for the great transformation from a relationship-based society into a rule-based society, discussed later in the chapter.

Law, social norm and economic development

As was emphasized earlier, a feature of the EADM is that explicit law plays a minor part in socioeconomic life while informal institutions like social norms played a major role. This phenomenon can be explained in light of the theory of the interlinked relational contract.

From the perspective of institutions (such as democracy and rule of law), authoritarian governments have no incentive to implement the rule of law under interlinked institutional arrangements (industrial policies), since they need discretion to intervene in the economy and coordinate behavior; formal institutions restrict flexibility in economic policy-making.

At early stages of economic development, effective governance often takes the form of self-enforcing interlinked relational contracts and the role of rule of law is limited due to the reason that with interlinked relational contracts, agents' decision-making is forward-looking, taking account of future interactions. In contrast, legal judgment is often backward-looking. Moreover, since transactions are interlinked, legal judgments cannot always take into account complex contractual interlinkage. Given all this, agents may rationally choose not to go to court. Only when markets are sufficiently complete does the rule of law become essential to economic development.

As discussed before, interlinked and relational contracts tend to generate multiple equilibria. Besides authorities (such as the government) who help to pick an efficient equilibrium, social conventions, norms and cultural traditions also act as coordination mechanisms, or "focal points" in the sense of Schelling (1960).[6]

Take the lifetime employment system and the main bank system in Japan as an example. Under the lifetime employment system, white collars and some blue collars at large corporations enjoy lifetime employment. In this

Table 6.1 International comparison of legal systems (1997)

	USA	UK	Germany	France	Japan
Number of legal practioners	945,508	82,653	111,315	35,695	19,733
per 100,000	*352.5*	*158.3*	*135.7*	*61.3*	*15.7*
Number of lawyers	906,611	80,868	85,105	29,395	16,368
per 100,000	*339.87*	*154.89*	*103.77*	*50.15*	*13.0*
Number of judges	30,888	3,170	20,999	4,900	2,093
per 100,000	*11.6*	*6.07*	*25.6*	*8.4*	*1.7*

Source: Saiko Saibansho, *On the Legal System of the 21st Century*[7]

employment relationship employers and employees all expect that employees will continuously work at a company until the mandatory retirement age. When the employment relationship starts, an employee's salary is lower than his or her contribution to productivity. But at a later stage of the employee's career, the salary exceeds his or her contribution to productivity. As part of the compensation package, biannual bonuses are related to performance, but not very closely. Pension plans are not transferable and labor mobility is highly restricted. In this case, the relationship between employer and employee is a typical relational contract in which rights and obligations of both parties are implicit and cannot be enforced by law.

The main bank system is another social norm in Japan's economic system. In fact, a main bank is not an organization established according to law and its role has not been defined through explicit rules or regulations. An important aspect of the commercial ideology of the main bank system is the shared expectation, among the bank, its borrowers, the firms affiliated to them, and the government, that the bank will avoid foreclosure and instead informally restructure bankrupt firms. Due to the existence of this norm, banks tend to bear more loss than is required by the bankruptcy law. Although the main banks have a certain priority of claims for loans, they voluntarily give the right to other lending banks. The whole main bank system is supported by a bunch of norms that encourage the bank to help financially weak firms (at least those firms that have the potential to regain liquidity and make a profit), in return for an informal commitment of the government to prevent the main bank from being bankrupt. There are many relational contracts in Japan's economy. Table 6.1 shows that even towards the end of the 1990s, the legal system still played a minor role in Japan's economy compared with legal systems of other countries. South Korea and Taiwan were faced with similar situations.

Transition of the East Asian Developmental Model

Interestingly, the interlinked relational institutional arrangements that appeared at an early stage of development in East Asia laid the foundations for their future unraveling and the emergence of a new system based on the rule of law.

Theoretically, economic development unravels interlinked relational contracts through specialization effects and market thickness effects. With larger market extent and division of labor, transactions once carried out through interlinked relational contracts can be brought to specialized markets. Moreover, the frequency and volume of transactions made on specialized markets will be higher; that is, the markets are "thicker", reducing the search cost for trading partners. The proliferation of outside options in specialized markets makes the enforcement of interlinked relational contracts increasingly difficult. As a consequence, personal transactions gradually give way to impersonal transactions as economies develop.

With these two effects, the necessary conditions for the success of industrial policies discussed earlier in the chapter change. First, the government's authority and the effectiveness of industrial instruments may change. With the expansion of credit and other markets, firms don't rely on as much government support as before. As pointed out by studies of the Japanese economy, "the government doesn't have resources to influence firms' decisions any more. This is especially true for large corporations that seldom depend on subsidies now. When carrot (incentive) was reduced, value of the government to the receiver (firms) also decreased" (Eads and Yamamura 1987).[8] Similar situations appeared in South Korea and Taiwan. Thus, at a certain stage of economic development, the second condition for effectiveness of industrial policies does not hold any more. Simultaneously, the relationship between development and innovation changes; at early stages of development, technology is far from the world technology possibility frontier, which means it suffices to learn and exploit technologies developed in foreign countries. The key issue facing these countries is how to mobilize resources, and hence government can play a vital role. But later, at the innovation-based development stage, research and development becomes increasingly important because the technology needed for further economic growth is at the world frontier. Lacking knowledge of advanced technology, the government now can hardly make and implement appropriate industrial policies; decentralized resource allocation becomes the better option.

From the perspective of politics, at the early stages of economic development, consensus is easily reached about the importance of economic development because development is a first priority for almost everyone. Thus social target is centered on economic growth. With the full development of the economy, people's preferences get more diverse. They begin to demand various public goods and legal rights. Social consensus about economic growth does not exist any longer. For instance, since the oil crisis starting in late 1960s, and especially after 1973, consensus about economic growth began to waver in Japan. Criticism of environmental problems and the problem of work stress was put forward. The distribution of the fruits of economic growth also concerned the public. People asked for better social amenities. Subsidies provided to some industries and interest groups began to receive more and more criticism. Many people started to ask whether rapid growth imposed high social costs. The disappearance of the social consensus had a negative influence on the position of the Japanese Liberal Democratic Party in the Diet (Eads and Yamamura 1987). Increased demand for justice and equality accelerated economic liberalization and the transformation from authoritarian governance to democracy and rule of law. In South Korea, the middle class emerged with economic development. Since the inauguration of President Roh Tae-woo in 1988, the political democratization process has been driven by the labor movement. Non-governmental organizations in Taiwan grew with economic development during the 1980s, especially those representing the middle class (for example, consumer protection and environmentalist organizations, associations for workers and peasants and so on) (Pang 1997). With social and economic development, the political process will reflect the rights of different social groups, and thus democratization becomes the historical trend.

From the perspective of the international environment, policy instruments used directly by the government (such as control of the domestic credit market, the direct allocation of investment) and indirectly (import and export quotas, weak anti-trust laws, favorable conditions for government procurement, etc.) met with great pressure in the context of globalization. For example, import quotas applied to 466 categories of items in Japan in 1962, but under pressure from the IMF and because of the GATT, the number of categories of items with import quotas has gradually decreased. Moreover, subsidies and favorable conditions have been cancelled under pressure from international organizations. In South Korea and Taiwan, similar situations occurred.

In these East Asian economies, deregulation and economic liberalization began at certain stages of economic development. Inclusive economic growth reduced the income gap and created a large middle class, which made the political democratization process more smooth and consolidated. However, because not all institutions shifted at the same pace, an institutional vacuum appeared in certain areas. Japan fell into economic stagnation from the late 1980s, and a financial crisis erupted in East Asia in late 1990s: both signs of an institutional vacuum, as has also documented by Li (2003).

General lessons from the EADM

The EADM offers many insights into economic development and institutional changes. A general idea we can draw from the EADM is that the role of government is a function of the economic development stage: at an early stage of development, government may adopt a series of policies to make up for missing markets and support market development; at stages with a high level of economic output and a sound market system, the government should withdraw from direct intervention and create a level field for market competition. At a certain point in the development process, political transition is needed to support the creation of democratic institutions and the rule of law. Specifically, the following lessons can be drawn from the EADM.

The importance of equal initial endowments

Egalitarian land reform started before economic take-off in the big East Asia economies. The reforms created equal economic conditions for people and gave widespread access to the fruits of economic growth, which made it easier for the government to implement pro-growth policies. Moreover, the formation of a large middle class laid the basis for a smooth transition to consolidated democracy.

A glance at developing countries in Africa and Latin America shows that the equality of initial endowments led to divergent development trajectories. In Africa and Latin America, initial economic inequality rendered social policies benefiting all the people (Pareto improvement) impossible. For instance, agricultural policies in many African countries seem to foster economic development by government intervention, but they are actually used to gain support from elite groups and benefit government officials, who support the government (Bates 1981). This is also the case with Latin America, where inequality in initial endowments led to a large income gap which made it difficult for the government to maintain autonomy and adopt long-term policies conducive to inclusive growth. Also, Latin American democracies are not consolidated. Left-wing governments tend to apply high rates of tax to redistribute wealth, which creates dissatisfaction among social elites (rich people) who then attempt to destabilize such governments. When they succeed in controlling the government, representatives of elites tend to adopt low tax rates favoring the elites. Then the poor people get dissatisfied and the left wing attempts to regain the power. Thus a vicious political cycle is observed in these countries.

The role of government as a function of the stages of economic development

The EADM shows that authoritarian governments can contribute to economic success at an early stage of development. In particular, due to limited market extent or missing markets at this stage, interlinked institutional arrangements (e.g. industrial policies) between the government and entrepreneurs (and/or other social groups) can substitute for complete markets. At the stage of investment-based economic development, interlinked relational contracts can help mobilize resources and foster development. The basic mechanism of the interlinked relational contract is that of long-term games on multiple dimensions. Transactions between agents tend to be multiplex and interlinked. Effective policies can internalize externalities and make up for missing markets. In addition, these types of games have multiple equilibria and thus coordination is very important. The more important coordination is, the greater the government's role will be. But with economic development and completeness of markets, multiplex relationships will unravel.

From the perspective of transaction costs, self-enforcing relational contracts are an economizing measure because they avoid the high set-up costs associated with formal institutional infrastructure. Thus, for early stages of economic development, relational governance is an "appropriate institution". However, with further economic development and market completion, diseconomies set in, and formal institutions that allow for economies of scale and endogenous technological progress come to the fore. Rule-based governance now becomes the "appropriate institution".

Timing and sequencing for economic liberalization

The proposition that the role of government is a function of the economic development stage implies that the government should withdraw from substantial economic intervention at a certain point in time during the development process. Therefore, the timing and sequencing of economic liberalization and opening up, either domestic or international, matters a lot for sustainable growth.

There is an apparent difference between the EADM and practice of Latin American countries as far as economic liberalization is concerned. In East Asian countries or regions, economic opening up and liberalization started when the market system and economic organizations at home were already fairly developed. In Latin America, most countries were engulfed in the capitalist world system before the domestic market system was sufficiently strong (Evans 1987). Large amounts of foreign investment surged into Latin American countries and investors formed powerful interest groups, which dominated the political process in these countries. As a result, relatively weak domestic organizations and capital were overwhelmed by strong foreign groups and the government's autonomy and state capacity was weak (Pang 1997). This failure of the government reflects the consequences of economic liberalization in the absence of well-developed domestic markets.

Timing for political transition

At a certain stage in economic development, the role of the government needs to change, and this always happens through political democratization. Political democratization is a natural result of inclusive economic growth under the EADM. A case in point is Taiwan. The Democratic Progressive Party (DPP) was founded in Taiwan in 1986. The Nationalist Government leader Chiang Ching-kuo recognized its legal status in the same year and lifted the ban on political parties, and a general election was held the next year. South Korea followed the same pattern. The military government led by Park Chung-hee in the 1960s and 1970s was basically an authoritarian government. After Roh Tae-woo became president in 1988, political democratization began.

Timely political democratization helps prevent the formation of coalitions between economic powers, political powers and interest groups that might obstruct economic development by exacerbating social injustice. The logic is simple: favorable industrial policies adopted by the government at early stages foster the development of some sectors and industries, creating rents for these groups. Democratization before interest groups become too powerful is necessary for sustainable growth. Therefore democratization usually goes hand in hand with economic liberalization (the break-up of monopoly and deregulation). In particular, at an early stage of economic development in East Asia, the centralized economic system and barriers to entry promoted long-term investment. But when economies arrive at the innovation-based growth stage, monopolized market structures restrict free entry and undermine technological innovation and future economic development.

At the early stages of economic development, self-enforcing interlinked relational contracts (either between government and firms or between firms) sustain socioeconomic life. When markets are small at the early stages of development, relationship-based contracts provide a more cost-effective governance structure than formal contracts (democratization and the rule of law). But with a deepening division of labor and expansion of the market, relationship-based contracts gradually give way to formal institutions enforced by third parties.

The relationship between economic development and institutional change can be summarized in Figure 6.1.

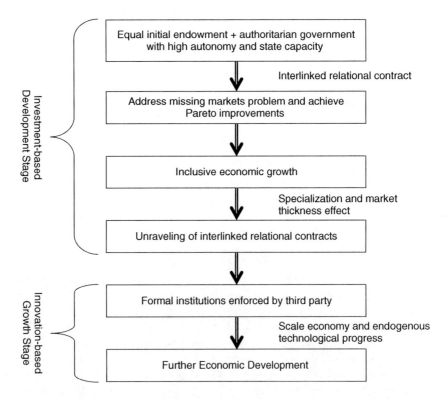

Figure 6.1 Economic development and institutional change under the EADM.

Lessons for China's transition

Economies of the EADM, most of which were still undeveloped agricultural economies (Korea and Taiwan, for example) in the 1940s, achieved rapid inclusive economic development and political democratization after World War II. The EADM created a miracle in the history of human development. Since reform and opening up began in 1978, China has been working another economic wonder with a staggering growth rate. There are some similarities between China's miracle and the miracle of the EADM. In particular, in the absence of sound market systems, interlinking institutional arrangements between government, economic organizations and economic agents achieved Pareto improvement (Wang and Li 2008). There are also differences between the development model of China and the EADM. The following key differences may shed some light on China's future trajectory.

Factor markets reform

One characteristic of the EADM is the egalitarian reform of factor markets, especially the land market, before economic take-off. Equal endowments arising from factor market reform is the key to inclusive economic growth and consolidated democratization. Looking wider, we find that the difference in development paths of North America and South America can also be attributed to differences in endowment distribution. Initial distribution of factors (especially land) was relatively even among people in North America, and people have an incentive to invest in human capital. In contrast, initial endowment was highly unequal in South America and people with little land had low bargaining power in society and low share of the benefits from economic growth, which means that they have little incentive to invest in human capital. This has contributed to the big divergence between the development in North and South America (Engerman and Sokoloff 2000).

Different from North America's experience and the EADM, China's reform occurs without egalitarian ownership of land and other factors. Although goods markets have been liberalized in China, liberalization of factor markets is yet to come. For example, in urban areas, land, nominally state owned, is actually monopolized by local government. Due to the *hukou* (residence permit) system, labor flow between rural and urban areas is strictly limited, which creates an undeveloped labor market. Considering the fact that private firms have negligible profit margin in the labor-intensive industries that are highly competitive, high prices of factors due to state monopoly have a negative influence on the development of firms and widen the income gap between different industries.

All these lagging reforms in factor markets have created special interest groups, including urban elites and government agencies, which constitute barriers to further economic liberalization. In theory, there are two possible scenarios. One is that the relational contract unravels when some specialized markets are well developed. The other is that the economy is trapped in relational contracting and arm's length markets cannot be well developed. Either of the two systems, namely, reciprocal contracting and arm's length contracting, is self-sustaining. Which one finally prevails depends on the interaction between market dynamics and the interlinked relational arrangements. In particular, as long as the total surplus from the interlinked relational arrangements is less than the total surplus from specialized markets, both politicians and entrepreneurs have no incentive to deviate from the relationship. In that case, the factor markets cannot be liberalized. This will in turn undermine the growth of the economy and increase the income gap, creating barriers to political democratization in the future. In the long run, as interlinked arrangements unravel, profound socioeconomic and political changes may occur. In this sense, China still has a long way to go towards a full modernization.

Aside from factor market reform lagging behind, there is asymmetry between reform in rural areas and in urban areas. Although urban residents don't have land ownership, they own the property established on the land. Since the land's value can be "capitalized" into the price of real estate, land ownership actually belongs to urban property owners and is transferable. In rural areas, however, residents don't have land ownership, either *de jure* or *de facto*. This widens the income gap between people in cities and in villages. The development of the labor market and the credit market is also asymmetric between cities and villages. Cities enjoy higher labor mobility and more credit resources than villages. This also contributes to the income gap between urban and rural areas. Another source of the income gap is that imperfect factor market reform leaves room for the corruption of government officials who have real control of the factors. China's income Gini coefficient is close to 0.5, much higher than that in the EADM. It follows that a key element in further reform is to reduce the income gap through factor market reform and other reforms.

Domestic economic liberalization and deregulation

Under the EADM, opening up occurs when there is a well-functioning domestic market system. Historically, other developed countries (European or American) followed the same pattern (Chang 2002). In contrast, economic liberalization happens without a sound market system at home in China. In this respect, China is more like countries in Latin America. Moreover, in many economic sectors of China, foreign investment is more welcome than private capital at home. While this kind of discrimination may have created some positive effects on GDP growth, it has caused certain domestic distortions, among which the entry barriers to many industries for the Chinese private sector is prominent. In the next decade or so, China should create a level playing field for all firms in China, in terms of entry, regulation and taxation.

As in the EADM, the Chinese government has a certain number of giant SOEs, monopolizing financial institutions, energy, natural resources, telecommunications and other so-called "key" industries. These industries not only create inefficiencies, but have also contributed substantially to income inequality in

China (Chen *et al.* 2010). Therefore, deregulation is vital for both efficiency and equity.

Timing for democratization and rule of law

The interlinked relational contract is an appropriate institution for the early stages of economic development with limited market extent. However, further economic development involves larger market extent and a more complete market system, which calls for formal institutions enforced by a third party. Good timing of this great transformation is needed for sustainable economic growth and human development. As has been shown in the case of the EADM, equality is very important for a consolidated democratization. It is also imperative for China to bring down the high income inequality before and during the political transition. It may be more feasible and practical to phase in an independent judicial system before the establishment of a fully fledged voting-based democracy.

7 Costs and benefits of relational contracting in China's transition

The last 35 years have witnessed great changes in China's economy and society. This chapter attempts to explore the social foundations of China's market-oriented transition and to further unravel the "China paradox": sustained economic growth without a formal institutional infrastructure – a sound legal system, well-defined property rights and an efficient financial system – since reform and opening up in the late 1970s. Naturally this leads us to search for the alternative informal mechanisms underlying the transition.

This chapter argues that the transition from a planned economy to a market-oriented economy requires market completion and perfection, which has important implications for economic governance. In particular, during China's transition thus far, informal institutions based on relational contracting[1] have made up for missing or imperfect markets and formal institutions.

With the further development of China's economy, the cost of relational contracting has grown increasingly high due to a diseconomy of scale, which arises from small-scale transactions that are completed using relational contracts. Inequality is a consequence of relational contracting, which encourages social segregation, specifically the division between "insiders" and "outsiders". Most importantly, if personal connections are embedded in the network of sociopolitical power, China's income gap will widen, leading to more resource misallocation and increased social inequality.

This chapter shows how the early stages of China's economic transition have caused relational contracts and interlinked arrangements to become effective substitutes for missing and imperfect markets. Transactions based on relational contracts may distort the emerging market mechanism, which in turn undermines further transition to a modern society. Specifically, relational contracting prevents the development of arm's length transactions and formal institutions, which is conducive to scale economy. In order for formal institutions to emerge, China's market economy must be decoupled from its sociopolitical powers. In this regard, there are two possible future scenarios of China's economic transition. (1) China's markets are so developed that they are dis-embedded from sociopolitical powers. (2) China's markets are less developed and embedded in sociopolitical powers, a trend that is characterized by many developing countries.

The next section contains a historical account of the relation-based society of China. This is followed by a section contextualizing relational contracts within China's economic transition. A theoretical account of relational contracting in China's economic transition is then provided, and an analysis of how economic development will unravel relation-based governance. The final section takes stock and looks ahead.

Relational society in China: a historical account

There are historical rationales for relation-based governance in China. As we will see, the relational transaction is a natural response to China's specific economic structure and political structure. Economically, China has been an agricultural society with low levels of labor mobility and division of labor, which has caused people living in the same communities to form long-term relationships.

In particular, when markets are incomplete, as is the case in many developing economies, contractual relationships between agents are not just relational, but also multiplex. A typical case of this type of contractual relationship exists between a landlord and his tenant in an agrarian society. The tenant usually pays his rent in kind as agreed upon in the contractual relationship. In addition, the landlord and tenant may share exposure to agriculture risks through a sharecropping arrangement, and in some cases the landlord will offer credit to the tenant. Thus, the same pair of parties interacts in multiple personalized markets (land, credit, insurance, labor and product), making their relationship both relational and multiplex. By contrast, in economies with more complete markets, people will transact with other agents in separate specialized markets. For instance, in these economies, farmers share risk with insurance companies.

Interlinked transactions are commonly observed in rural China. For example, family A may ask family B to lend a hand in building houses without financial payment. When harvesting time arrives, family B may collect on this favor by asking family A for assistance in harvesting crops. This type of interlinked transaction effectively addresses the issue of a missing labor market for rural construction and harvesting.

One advantage of interlinked contracts is that they mitigate the problem of moral hazard and adverse selection that may exist in a single market by offsetting losses in one market with gains in another. In other words, unviable transactions in a single market may become viable with interlinked contracts since people care more about the net surplus in the bundled transactions. Therefore, interlinked contracts can enlarge the feasible set of relational contracts (Wang 2007). In societies with missing markets, interlinked contracts can make up for specialized markets and achieve Pareto improvements. Historically, there are at least three particular foundations for China's relation-based governance, as follows.

Social networks based on extended family

Families have played an essential role in traditional Chinese agricultural society. As recently as 1953, 90 percent of the Chinese population lived in rural areas (Chao 2006). In such a society, families and extended families were the basic organizations around which production, consumption and other economic activities were centered. Economic exchanges mainly took place at the local level of villages and townships, a trend that arose from missing specialized markets and ultimately encouraged transactions between the agents to be relational and interlinked. This governance was in line with the limited scale economy of agricultural society and enforceable due to the repeated interactions of the agents. Except for a short unsuccessful period during the Mao era when the agricultural sector was divided into communes, families and extended families have been the basic agricultural production unit.

Centralized hierarchy in polity

China's political system has been based on a centralized hierarchy system since the Qin dynasty, and during its agrarian era, dual governance has been the norm. The state has a strong control over higher level jurisdictions, while at the local level, landed gentry have an informal authority within their localities through community-wide networks.

Since 1949 and the beginning of Communist China, a centralized hierarchy system has been used to allocate resources based on planning and rationing. This system was used instead of a well-functioning market system and over time has caused personal connections to play a critical role in obtaining scarce resources.

Low level of labor mobility

In 1958 the Chinese government adopted the *hukou* system, a residential permit system that places restrictions on mobility, particularly between the rural and urban sectors. Many suspect that *hukou* is largely responsible for the rural–urban divide that exists in China today. In the rural sector, the grassroots organizations are village governments. In the urban sector, work units (*danwei*) are the basic organization. Due to the repression of markets, *danwei* became an encompassing state-sponsored organization that provided housing, medical care and other life-long services to people belonging to work units. In effect, *danwei* provided further disincentives for mobility within both the urban and rural sectors during the planning era.

Low mobility and absence of markets make the relational contract a feasible and rational choice for people in both rural and urban sectors. In the rural sector, village community-based interlocking relationships act as an effective substitute for missing markets, and in the urban sector, the work unit system is essentially an interlinked relational contract between the state and the urban workers. The next section elaborates on these points.

The role of relational governance in China's transition

Transition from a central planning economy to a market economy is a process of market completion. In the process, interlinked relational governance as transitional governance has played an important role.

The role of families

In rural areas, as the basic economic and social unit, families contributed much to the success of the Household Responsibility System (HRS), a family-based farming system under collective land ownership. In strong contrast with People's Commune System, under HRS, family members have little incentive to shirk or take a free ride on other members. Thus, at early stages of reform and the opening up of China's economy, this new system fostered the development of rural sectors. Under the HRS, land and other means of production are used by families. Family members share the consumption of the family's output. In a social context, an individual is not completely independent and family members take responsibility for each other's behavior. This system not only improves productivity, it constitutes an effective risk-sharing mechanism. In urban sectors, the family also plays an important role in transition. Take laid-off workers as an example. Without transfer and support from other family members, these workers could scarcely withstand the risks of unemployment and other hazards that they are exposed to during such a transition.

One important form of risk sharing and consumption smoothing within families is transfers between generations and across family members of the same generation. Primary education in rural sectors is a good example of intergenerational transfers. During 1994–99 much of the financial burden of primary education in rural areas fell on families. Before the rural tax and fee reform, township governments were responsible for most compulsory education financing. As a result, families also contributed to precautionary savings. Table 7.1 illustrates household savings before the transition and a couple of

Table 7.1 Household savings in China

Sector	Ratio to national saving
1957	5.3%
Urban	5.7%
Rural	4.9%
1982	20%
Urban	4.8%
Rural	26.8%
1984	24.7%
Urban	7.9%
Rural	32%

Source: Qian (1988).

Table 7.2 Percentage receiving instrumental and financial support by source and rural/urban residence

	Instrumental support		Financial support	
Source	*Rural area*	*Urban area*	*Rural area*	*Urban area*
From children	60.8	53.3	43.8	33.5
From other sources	2.8	4.4	9.7	5.4
From both sources	6.0	3.8	29.1	13.0
From neither sources	30.4	38.5	17.4	48.1
Total	100	100	100	100

Source: Zimmer and Kwong (2003).

years immediately after the transition. Comparison between urban sectors and rural sectors is also shown. It can be inferred that the savings rate has been increasing since China's economic transition, particularly in rural areas.

In China, a family's role in risk sharing is also demonstrated in support of those in old age. Children usually contribute certain income and health care to their elderly parents. In both the urban and rural sectors, a substantial proportion of daily care for aged people is given by their children. The ratio is 60.8 percent in rural areas and 53.3 percent in urban areas. On average children pay 43.8 percent of their parents' costs in rural areas and 33.5 percent in urban areas. The lower urban ratio is partly due to the fact that urban residents usually have higher security pensions (see Table 7.2). Obviously children play an important role in providing income smoothing for aged parents.

Community level networks

A family's ability to deal with problems of missing or imperfect markets is rather limited. When the whole family is subject to certain risk or shock, the limitations of a single family to withstand such events will surface. Furthermore, a family would be unable to meet demands for large amounts of money and to solve other problems. Social interaction on the community level can mitigate problems. It enables families and individuals to allocate resources in a broader scope, which fosters production, consumption and other social interactions on a larger scale. Tables 7.3 and 7.4 show two-level mutual insurance (within and without the village) in Zouping county, Shandong province, indicating that cooperation at the community level can improve welfare.

Table 7.3 depicts mutual insurance in the form of consumption smoothing among community members. For insurance provided among family members, the coefficient of variation of consumption, as a measure of consumption risk, is as high as 29.5. The coefficient of variation of consumption can be reduced by 15.5 if a mutual insurance arrangement can be achieved at the level of village community. If the mutual insurance is further extended to the county level, the

Table 7.3 The potential for risk sharing

Types	Coefficient of variation
Autarky (consumption = income)	29.5
Village-level risk sharing	14.0
County-level risk sharing	5.4

Source: Morduch and Sicular (2001: 224).

Table 7.4 Transfers received inside versus outside the village

	Households receiving transfers from within the village	Households receiving transfers from outside the village	All households
Percentage of observations	23.6%	9.8%	100%
Average value of within village transfers	150.3	79	35.5
Average value of outside village transfers	66.4	307.5	30.1
Average household income	1499.2	1352.8	1277

Source: Morduch and Sicular (2001: 226).

coefficient can be reduced to only 5.4.[2] Table 7.3 differentiates two levels of mutual insurance: within and across villages. Data in Table 7.3 is measured in currency unit. It shows that 23.6 percent of families sampled received transfers from within the village community, with each family getting 150.3 *yuan*. It also shows that 9.8 percent of families sampled received transfers from outside the village, with each family getting 307.5 *yuan*.

Investigation of different forms of transfers in Table 7.4 is enlightening. Morduch and Sicular (2001) examined transfers in kind such as meat and food as well as pure cash among villagers, but not labor transfer. They also showed that labor transfer is an important form of mutual help. About 19.2 percent of the families surveyed experienced labor transfers.

Aside from informal insurance mechanisms, informal finance based on relationship played an important role where a person or private enterprise would find it difficult to obtain a loan from the banking sector. Informal finance is a form of borrowing from relatives, friends and acquaintances. Tsai (2002) examined informal finance by collecting data from southern and northern cities in China. Tsai's findings, included in Table 7.5, show that many people (above 50 percent in northern China) are satisfied with borrowing from informal finance channels. During the period in question, informal financing met 75 percent of the demand for loans in the private sector. Thus, there is evidence that informal finance played a pivotal role in the development of China's private sector.

Partly because businesses tend to resort to family support for financing, labor employment, and so on, China's private businesses usually take the form of

Table 7.5 Informal finance in China

Area	Proportion of people who borrowed	Average amount (yuan)	Average duration (months)	Average interest rate
North China	59.0	18,863	10.5	0.32%
South China	43.6	43,003	6.1	1.14%

Source: Tsai (2002: 57).

family firms. As a result, China boasts a large number of family firms which in essence are a form of business organization associated with family, partly due to missing or imperfect markets.

Social interaction between families, communities and local governments

During China's economic transition, aside from these voluntary relational transactions, there are also interactions between family, community and government, which are not necessarily based on explicit rules or laws. The township and village enterprise (TVE) is a typical case of such interaction.

At the early stages of transition, factor markets such as the credit market and the land market were either missing or far from perfect. In this context, TVEs arose as "an interlinked contract" between entrepreneurs and local governments across multiple markets (Wang and Li 2007). On the one hand, in the case of the imperfect factor market, entrepreneurs focused on establishing cooperative relationships with local governments who controlled resources and also granted property rights protection. On the other hand, local governments needed to address issues of revenue and employment through local economic development.

Due to the lack of financial markets, TVEs cannot easily obtain financing. Therefore, it is necessary for families, communities, and governments to form long-term relationships. In all, the investment to set up a new business consists of (1) fund pooling of original village teams, which accounts for 28.17 percent of the investment; (2) bank loans backed by village property, which accounts for 17 percent of investment; (3) bank loans guaranteed by village officials, which accounts for 11 percent of investment; (4) and loans guaranteed by governments, which accounts for 20.5 percent of investment. During the seventh "five-year plan" period, a report was issued that showed private firms (TVEs) receiving 15 percent of financing from their relatives and friends, and 1.9 percent of funding provided by employees themselves (Chen 1995). Similarly, land is owned collectively and there is no sound land market at the early stage of transition; entrepreneurs needed to develop a cooperative relationship with local governments for the favor of land use.

TVEs help local governments solve employment problems. In TVEs labor recruitment usually is done through collaboration between firm owners and local governments. After the implementation of the HRS, a large amount of surplus labor emerged in rural areas. Local governments were faced with unemployment problems, which became an important driver for establishing TVEs. In fact, about 40.5 percent of TVE workers were placed by local officials. Moreover, about 75 percent of TVE managers were assigned by leaders of township and village (Chen 1995).

Because TVEs are "an interlinked relational contract" between entrepreneurs and local governments, it is natural that the allocation of control rights and residual claims in a township and village enterprise are different from that in a standard business – these rights are divided between firms and governments.[3] Take rights of management as an example. In 13 important rights of management decision-making of TVEs, 33 percent of decisions are made solely by township governments, another 33 percent are jointly made by the government and the firm, and the remaining 34 percent are made independently by the firm (Chen 1995). In profit allocation, the government has received much more than it could by taxation and fee. Part of the profit share of the government is returned to society through public goods and service provision. TVEs themselves also take corresponding social responsibility in support primary education and public health. The remaining profit is usually equally allocated among workers.

Apart from TVEs, a form of organization started with cooperation between entrepreneurs, communities and local governments, where there were private firms seeking an identity of a state-owned or collectively owned enterprise through various means (for example, affiliated with a government organization or a state-owned company). These private businesses, in the form of a state-owned or collectively owned company (the so-called "red capped" enterprises), can have access to resources (financial resources, right to export, etc.) otherwise unavailable to private firms and enjoy more property rights protection from the government. Local government and related organizations can receive a lump sum of administrative charges and alleviate the unemployment problem by transferring some workers from state-owned companies to those affiliated private firms.

Like TVEs, "red capped" enterprises are a kind of transitional institutional organization in line with imperfect factor markets and insufficient private property protection during China's early transition. By the end of the 1990s, factor markets developed quickly and private property was better protected by constitution and other statutes, and this speeded up the transformation of TVEs into private firms and caused the disappearance of the "red capped" phenomena.[4]

Interlinked arrangements in the urban state sector

The market-oriented reform of state sectors is in essence a process of dismantling the planning system in general and Work Unit System in particular. Take the reform of state-owned enterprises (SOEs), for example. This reform concerns changes in multiple markets such as labor, education, medical care, insurance and housing. Historically employees got low pay, with the government provision of benefit packages and life employment. State-owned enterprises maintained interlinked relationships with their employees for a long time after the reform began. In particular, the *xiagang* arrangement ("stepping down from one's post"), where an employee, even when got laid off, was still entitled to a certain level of allowance, and other welfare programs. As evidenced in a survey (Development Research Center of State Council 2004), which elaborated on the costs of SOE restructuring, per capita payments of central government controlled SOEs amounted to 14,000 *yuan* while per capita payments of local government controlled SOEs amounted to 40,500 *yuan* (State Council 2005).

In conclusion, at the early stages of transition, due to incomplete markets of credit, insurance, land and labor, and weak protection for private property, there appeared a series of substitute cooperative relationships and institutional arrangements in rural sectors and in urban sectors, which has fostered economic development while reducing the cost of transition.

The role of relational governance in transition: a theoretical summary

During economic transition, due to missing markets and formal institutions, relational transactions provided a substitute for those missing institutions in the social economy. This section contains a brief theoretical summary of the roles of relational governance in China's transition.

Relational governance as an effective substitute for missing and imperfect markets

Transition is a process of dismantling the old institutions in the planning economy; some alternative mechanism is the key to the performance of transition before the market system is in place. The sequence of liberalization also matters. Since rural residents have more solid traditional networks than urban citizens, beginning the reform in rural areas was the best choice. Had the reform started with the urban sector, it could have brought more risk to the reform because the social network is weaker for urban residents and it could have been the case that formal and informal institutions were both missing. In rural areas, market-oriented reform progressed without breaking social networks, as discussed above.

The success of rural reform made urban reform relatively easy. The development of rural areas not only enlarged the markets for the industrialized products of cities, it supplied raw materials needed by cities and released cheap surplus labor for urban development. As discussed above, the urban reform beginning in 1984 did not break the social relationship based on the "work unit system" immediately. In the absence of a well-functioning labor market, credit and social security system, arrangement of labor, housing, medical care and financing, those work units (mostly state-owned enterprises) still kept close interlinked relationships in labor, housing, medical care and the like with their employees until the mid-1990s when many specialized markets came into being.

Relational governance as a self-enforcing substitute mechanism for formal institutions

Under "cold turkey" transition in Russia and other transition economies, the old regime was dismantled almost overnight and there was a long period of "institutional vacuum". To fill this vacuum, other forms of governance, like the mafia, appeared. In contrast, one feature of China's gradualism is that market-oriented reform advanced without major changes of original political and social structure.

Considering the rather limited function of the formal legal system during economic transition, China's economic transition was based on informal institutions. The underlying rationale is that interlinked relational transactions involve long-running multiplex interests that are hard to verify and enforce in courts and the agents may rationally not resort to court. A survey of 2002 shows that even in the Yangtze river delta, where the market economy is more developed, many firms chose to settle their disputes by direct negotiation, through the intervention of local government or in a private way (by local business partners) (see Table 7.6).

Relational governance is cost-effective when market extent is limited

Relational contracts are self-enforcing through long-term relationships between fixed agents. It only requires that local information is common knowledge to both parties and they have shared expectations. Transactions based on formal institutions require that relevant information be verifiable by a third party (for example, the court). In addition, high fixed costs are needed for institutional infrastructure.[5] Therefore, informal institutions through self-enforcing relational contracts and formal institutions enforced through courts have their comparative advantages.

At the early stages of development and transition, when market extent is limited, relational governance is a more appropriate institution in that it has lower requirements on information structure (no third-party verification is needed)

Table 7.6 Perceived most efficient conflict resolutions in the Yangtze delta (%)

Resolutions	Foreign firms	SOEs	Private firms	Collective firms
Negotiation	46.6	52.5	56.4	54.9
Court	37.5	36.0	35.6	33.3
Local government intervention	17.8	15.8	8.6	9.8
Private means	8.7	5.0	11.8	5.9
No way	5.5	6.5	5.7	5.9
Otherwise	4.0	2.2	4.9	3.9
Total	120.2	118.0	123.0	113.7

Note: Due to multiple choices, the totals are more than 100 percent.

Source: Wang, Yujian *et al.* (2007: 154).

and it incurs no fixed cost for the establishment of a legal system, which reduces transaction costs greatly (Li 2003). Because agents in a long-term relationship tend to have transactions in multiple "interlinked" markets, the average transaction cost is further lowered (namely, there is scope economy with interlinked contracts). Interlinked contracts expand the feasible set of transactions. If transactions are not interlinked and one party suffers a loss in a single transaction, then he may simply quit; but if transactions are interlinked, loss in a single transaction can be offset by gains from other transactions, which makes quitting an undesirable option.

The above discussion can shed some light on the institutional foundations for the different performance of transition economies.[6] The radical reform of Russia destroyed the basis of the traditional system almost overnight, without establishing effective formal institutions within a short time. The institutional void caused social anomie. China's gradualism to a large extent maintained interlinked contracts of the traditional social and political system, which partly accounts for the Chinese economic miracle after transition (Wang 2005, 2006, 2007).

Economic development and the gradual dismantling of relational governance

Ironically, although relational governance has been fostering economic development and marketization, it has also been unraveling governance gradually. Specialized markets have taken over most of the functions originally performed by social networks like families and communities. And the higher level of labor mobility shortens the time horizon of interaction among agents. As is elaborated below, in many dimensions, the traditional relational society has been gradually dismantled.

Marketization and traditional social networks

With the advancement of marketization and some social policies (like the one-child policy), the interlinked relationship at the levels of family, community and local government has been weakened.

China's family structure is undergoing substantial change and there is a clear trend of a weakening of the familial network. Nuclear families composed of parents and children are the major family structure in cities, towns and villages. The ratio of nuclear families to all families is the highest in cities, then towns, and lowest in villages. Historically, nuclear families constituted less than half of all families in the 1960s; now they are more than half and the number of composite families has been decreasing (Wang 2006). Also, among nuclear families, the ratio of working, childless couples ("DINK" families) has been increasing during transition. Families were made still smaller due to higher college admission rates. The average number of members of families has dropped from 4.41 in 1982 to 3.96 in 1990 and 3.44 in 2000 (Wang 2006).

However, although the social network at the level of family has been weakened, it will take quite a long time for the profound influence of smaller families on economic life to play out. Even within a nuclear family, mutual insurance capability was weakened due to fewer family members than before. Minimized families will be less capable of providing for and taking care of aged people (Wang 2006b). The weakening of the family network will expose individuals to more risk in the absence of specialized insurance markets, credit markets and the social security system.

As previously mentioned, at the level of community and government, the success of TVEs depended on good relationships between entrepreneur, community and government, who have interlinked transactions in multiple markets in contexts where specialized markets such as financial markets and land markets were missing. The government provided political protection and favorable policies, or other public services, and in return the government received a share of the surplus from the development of TVEs and higher levels of employment were achieved. However, the development of specialized markets impaired the advantage of TVEs and entrepreneurs did not have to keep close relationships with community and government as before. In addition, with a more developed labor market in place and hence higher labor mobility, people tend to work outside of their own communities. All this led to a dismantling of many TVEs in the mid-1990s (Wang and Li 2008). And since the mid-1990s, the privatization of state sectors and marketization of medical care, education and housing in cities have been advanced by the government. As a result, the traditional work unit system has gone, and with it the social relationship centered around those work units. Cities have changed from being a community of people with long-term relationships into an anonymous world.

Labor mobility and traditional networks

The dismantling of the close relationship associated with families, communities and governments in transition has been briefly discussed. The effects of enhanced labor mobility on the traditional social networks are now highlighted, and to begin with we look at the history of China's labor mobility. Table 7.7 illustrates labor mobility in China according to the destinations in a recent 20-year period. At the early stages of transition, destinations of the labor force were mostly villages and rural towns, which corresponded to the booming of TVEs. But after the mid-1980s, an increasing number of workers moved to cities, and the ratio of migrants into villages and towns to all migrants was decreasing, although the trend experienced a temporary turnaround during 1995–2000.

Migration within villages and towns is related to the development of TVEs. The main wave of privatization of TVEs occurred during 1990–95. In fact, the labor force employed by TVEs accounted for 9.4 percent of rural labor in 1980, and the ratio increased to around 26 percent in 1995 and has stayed at that level ever since (Brooks and Tao 2003). In cities, on the other hand, the average annual employment rate was growing at 3 percent from 1990 even when

Table 7.7 Percentage of flow of in-migration to cities, towns and rural townships

Destination	1982–87	1985–90	1990–95	1995–2000
Cities	36.6	61.7	61.4	59.4
Towns	39.8	20.1	10.0	19.16
Rural areas	23.6	18.2	28.6	21.43

Source: Shi (2006).

there were large numbers of laid-off workers from SOEs (Shi 2006). Therefore, China's labor force experienced large-scale migration, with destinations changing from villages and towns to cities. This massive labor mobility during transition weakens the traditional social network of relational society and exposes the people to more risks.

Development as a process of unraveling interlinked and relational institutions

The dismantling of relational governance during China's economic transition and development can shed some light on relationships between economic development and institutional change in general. In particular, economic development has the following two effects on traditional institutions.

First is the specialization effect. When markets become more specialized and complete, personal transactions under interlinked contracts give way to arm's length transactions on the markets. For example, in rural areas, some services that used to be delivered in the form of mutual help are now replaced by those on specialized markets. Development is a process that unravels the interlinked contracts (Wang 2007).

Second is the market thickness effect. With the expansion of markets and deepening of the division of labor, the frequency and number of transactions on specialized markets keeps increasing (i.e. markets become "thicker"); this in turn attracts more buyers and sellers to join market transactions due to a lower search cost. Arm's length markets will dominate reciprocal exchange when the markets are thick enough (Kranton 1996).

As far as the link between development stage and governance is concerned, at the stage when market extent is small and the specialization level is low, relational governance is cost-effective in that it is self-enforcing and requires no set-up cost for formal institutional infrastructure. With economic development and market expansion, the cost of relational governance grows and formal institutions become more attractive. In other words, due to large fixed costs associated with formal institutions, transactions based on formal institutions enjoy an economy of scale (i.e. the more transactions, the lower average transaction cost). Therefore, the optimal institutional arrangement depends on the stage of economic development. We may conclude the general relationship between economic development and transaction institutions from Figure 7.1.

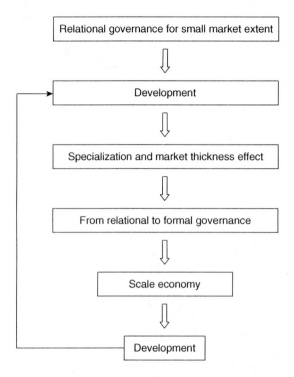

Figure 7.1 Dynamics of development and institutional change.

Generally speaking, economic development will transform a relational society to a society based on formal institutions through the specialization effect and the market thickness effect. This transformation will trigger further economic development, as indicated in Figure 7.1. In the words of Polanyi, this is the great transformation, from the equilibrium where economic relationship is embedded in social relationship to an equilibrium where social relationship is embedded in economic relationship (Polanyi 1957).

Concluding remarks

The final realization of the great transformation depends on whether the effects of specialization and market thickness work well. There are some forces against these two effects in China's current political and social structure, as discussed below.

Chinese-style federalism and market segmentation

In the last 35 years Chinese-style federalism has promoted economic growth through yardstick competition among jurisdictions under a strong central government. However, it has also led to beggar-your-neighbor competition, in the form of segmentation of markets and public services, which undermines economy of scale and the extent of markets. Therefore it constitutes an impediment to the great transformation. The key lies in the incompatibility of localism of local governments with the call for an integrated and specialized domestic market system. We may expect certain social anomie when there are no formal institutions in place while the traditional society is on the verge of breakdown.

Marketization embedded in sociopolitical powers

There are two possible future trajectories of China's market-oriented reform: (1) the markets are so developed that they will become decoupled from sociopolitical powers; (2) the markets are less developed and remain embedded in sociopolitical powers, as characterized by Latin American countries. Under gradual transition, the traditional power structure remains and the market value of powers has been "capitalized" during marketization. Therefore the markets are embedded in sociopolitical powers.

Some empirical studies on the effect of powers on income show that favorable political identity and social networks do improve income.[7] Because the markets are embedded in sociopolitical powers, there is a separation of "insiders" and "outsiders" in the process of policy-making, with insiders enjoying more power of resource allocation. From the dynamic perspective, people with more power can amass a fortune more quickly, and then they invest money in gaining more power, which exacerbates social polarity. Even worse, the trend of polarity can go on across generations.

Markets embedded in sociopolitical powers may hinder the transformation of relational society into a society based on formal institutions through the market thickness effect. If relational contracting prevails in socioeconomic transactions, the specialized market will become thinner due to high search cost. Reciprocal exchange will be a self-sustaining equilibrium (Kranton 1996). A typical example is the labor market. If people get their jobs through social relations, the labor market will become thin.

Turning to the relations between firms and governments, in jurisdictions with a higher ratio of private enterprises, private enterprises may in theory gain more by keeping good relations with government officials. A World Bank survey on the investment environment of 23 cities in China shows that it is indeed the case. In this survey, the ratio of the cost of bribing government officials and regulators to sales were measured. What merits our attention is that Shenzhen and Wenzhou, two cities with a high ratio of private firms, also have high abnormal payments (World Bank 2003).

Markets embedded in sociopolitical powers and social relations are perilous. The quandary of economic development in many less developed countries is related to a distorted resource allocation due to the fact that interest groups abuse powers in the process of resource allocation. The distortion not only jeopardizes social justice and economic efficiency, it thwarts efforts in effective social reform.

To avoid crony capitalism, China should prevent markets from being embedded in sociopolitical powers and social relationships.

The possibility of institutional vacuum

Previously we explored the case that marketization may dismantle relational society. And we also analyzed some hindrances to the transformation of a traditional society into a modern one. Ideally, when the economy develops to the extent that markets are relatively complete and market extent is large, formal institutions are adopted. But in reality, market maturity and formal institutions may not go hand in hand. The critical point where traditional society turns into modern society based on formal institutions is risky because it is the time when an institutional vacuum may occur since both traditional governance and modern governance may be absent. And economic crisis and political crisis may ensue.[8] Therefore, when economic development comes to a certain point, the timing for introducing formal institutions is essential.

Notes

1 Introduction

1 Autonomy means that the government is immune to the influence of interest groups and adopts economic policies that maximize social welfare.

2 Interlinking markets, relational contracts and economic transition

1 Braverman and Stiglitz (1982) provide a classic study of interlinking markets; for a survey on the literature on interlinked contracts, see Wang and Bao (2007).
2 Levin 2003 provides the single-market benchmark of relational contract. For a survey of the single-market relational contract, see Bolton and Dewatripont (2005).
3 The latter is typical moral hazard (hidden action).
4 Perfect public equilibrium (PPE) equilibrium is formally defined by Fudenberg and Maskin (1994).
5 By construction it can be shown that such equilibrium exists.
6 For alternative explanations, see Che and Qian (1998) and Weitzman and Xu (1993).
7 For the role of social capital in transition economies, see Stiglitz (1999).
8 Using similar argument, Li (2003) explains the cost and benefits of the East Asia model.

3 Markets, contracts and economic growth

1 There are two definitions of transaction cost in economics. Some economists refers to cost spent in product transaction (such as traffic cost, search cost, etc.) not included in the production process; some identify it with deadweight loss due to institutional reasons (e.g. moral hazard and adverse selection). The concept used here takes the former definition to characterize the change in the ratio of services sector in the economy.
2 It is interesting that our framework can well explain why the integration of Europe is the best in the world. In the knowledge economy age, European countries with similar development are strongly mutually complementary, which is why the integration level is higher in Europe than in North America (such as NAFTA).
3 For more detailed analysis of China's economic history using this framework, see Lu *et al.* (2007).

4 Interlinked contracts and development: where do we stand?

1 The intuition here could be simply interpreted as follows: landlords' income on the two markets is affected by the two variables of interest rate and wage. If contracts are signed separately, landlords would only be able to control the interest rate on the credit margin, and control the wage on the tenancy margin. Then the sum of the two

maximized income results separately from the two margins would be less or equal to the sum of the incomes by landlords directly maximized through the interlinked contracts.

2 Equivalent to $B = c_0$ in the above model.

3 The "fixed" here means that the sharecropping ratio agreed upon between landlords and tenants *ex ante* cannot be adjusted *ex post*. While traders and tenants usually decide *ex ante* on the trade volume rather than the prices, the prices here can be adjusted depending on the market environment.

4 This is due to the concavity of the tenant's utility function: reducing his consumption may lead to enhanced work incentive resulting from increased consumption.

5 The non-interlinked lenders can only establish uniform terms. But the interlinked lenders can establish different repayment terms in line with different trading contexts. The flexibility of the latter has better risk-sharing property.

6 The absolute value of the Arrow-Pratt coefficient is less than 1.

7 We generally assume that all new technologies share the features of high yields and high risk.

8 However, since the tenants' income is always kept at the reservation utility level, even if they obtain production credit, they are not likely to have an opportunity to purchase the land through the increased income and turn themselves into yeomen.

9 Li (2003) applies a similar framework to analyze the East Asian Development Model, as elaborated in Chapter 6.

5 Unraveling the Chinese miracle: a perspective of interlinked relational contracts

1 Basu's (2001) "core theorem" shows that in theory any exchange that can be enforced by formal contracts can also be enforced by social norms (i.e. informal contract). The logic here is that if legal provisions are not Nash equilibria in games, they cannot be enforced, but social norms are Nash equilibria in the real world.

2 For single-market relational contracts, see Levin (2003) or Bolton and Dewatripont (2005).

3 Actually, some anthropologists have already had this insight. For example, Bailey (1968) notes that: "the watershed between traditional society and modern society is exactly the distinction between single interest and multiplex relationships. The hallmark of modern society is the specialized role and the whole apparatus of its productive prosperity rests upon the division of labor between specialized roles".

4 For a classic formal treatment of interlinked contracts in agriculture, see Braverman and Stiglitz (1982).

5 Wang and Bao (2007) present a comprehensive survey on the theoretical literature on interlinked contract.

6 National leaders in China like Deng Xiaoping predicted the emergence of TVEs, which evolved out of the state plan.

7 In 1984, Chinese central government issued No. 4 document (*sihao wenjian*), formally recognizing and legalizing the TVEs and giving leeway for further development.

8 For other complementary views on TVEs, see Weitzman and Chenggang (1994), and Che and Qian (1998). For more institutional details, see Oi (1999).

9 See Kuang (1999).

10 For a detailed documentation of informal finance in China, see Tsai (2002).

11 See Kuang (1999), note 14.

12 From a talk by Zhou Xiaochuan on 16 April 2004. For more details, see: www.pbc. gov.cn/hanglingdaojianghua/.

13 For example, see Li (2003).

14 For a political economy account of Chinese transition, see Wang, Yongqin *et al.* (2007).

6 The East Asian Development Model reconsidered with implications for China

1 In this chapter Japan, Korea and Taiwan are mainly used as examples, since they are more representative given their size, while Hong Kong and Singapore are basically city economies.
2 For a good survey of the literature on aggregate features, especially on total factor productivity (TFP) in East Asian economies, see Lin and Ren (2006).
3 Edwards (1993) is a nice survey on trade and development.
4 Interestingly, Mulligan and Shleifer (2005) show that this point also holds in the United States empirically. They show that states with larger populations have more regulations.
5 The idea of industrial policy can be traced back to List (1841). For current advocacy, see Chang (2002).
6 Myerson (2004) also argues that justice is a focal point equilibrium in case of multiple equilibria.
7 See www.courts.go.jp/pre21/16/gif.
8 Gerschenkron (1962) also noticed that the same thing was observed in German industrialization. At early stages of industrialization, banks had more control over firms. Later on, firms had more bargaining power.

7 Costs and benefits of relational contracting in China's transition

1 "Relational contracting" and "relational governance" are used interchangeably in this chapter.
2 Note the risk sharing in the village community was among 16 villages.
3 For alternative explanation, see Weitzman and Xu (1993). They argue that the community-level cooperative culture played an important role.
4 For further analysis on TVEs, see Wang and Li (2008).
5 Interestingly, Mulligan and Shleifer (2005) also show this empirically. Using state-level data in the US, they show that states with larger populations have more regulation.
6 Stiglitz (1999) also underlines the importance of social capital in transition economies.
7 For instance, employing China's urban data, Knight and Yueh (2008) find that Communist Party membership substantially increased personal income in private firms.
8 For instance, Li (2003) argues that the East Asian financial crises in the late 1990s was due to the institutional vacuum between the two systems.

References

Acemoglu, Daron, Aghion, Philippe and Zilibotti, Fabrizio, 2006, "Distance to Frontier, Selection, and Economic Growth", *Journal of the European Economic Association*, 4(1): 37–74.

Akamatsu, K., 1962, "A Historical Pattern of Economic Growth in Developing Countries", *Journal of Developing Economies*, 1(1): 3–25.

Allen, F., 1985, "On the Fixed Nature of Sharecropping Contracts", *Economic Journal*, 95(377): 30–48.

Amsden, Alice H., 1989, *Asia's Next Giant: South Korea and Late Industrialization*. Oxford: Oxford University Press.

Aoki, M., Kim, H. and Okuno-Fujiwara, M. (eds), 1997, *The Role of Government in East Asian Economic Development: Comparative Institutional Analysis*. Oxford: Oxford University Press.

Baily, F. G., 1971, "The Peasant View of Bad Life", in T. Shanin (ed.), *Peasants and Peasant Societies*. Harmondsworth: Penguin.

Banerji, S., 1995, "Interlinkage, Investment and Adverse Selection", *Journal of Economic Behavior and Organization*, 28: 11–12.

Bardhan, P. K., 1980, "Interlocking Factor Markets and Agrarian Development: A Review of Issues", *Oxford Economic Papers*, 32: 82–98.

Bardhan, P. K., 1984, *Land, Labor and Rural Poverty: Essays in Development Economics*. New York: Columbia University Press.

Basu, K., 1983, "The Emergence of Isolation and Interlinkage in Rural Markets", *Oxford Economic Papers*, 35: 262–80.

Basu, K., 1984, *The Less Developed Economy*. Oxford: Blackwell.

Basu, K., 1990, *Agrarian Structure and Economic Underdevelopment*. Harwood Academic Publishers.

Basu, K., 2001, "The Role of Social Norms and Law in Economics: An Essay on Political Economy", in J. W. Scott and D. Keates (eds), *Schools of Thought*. Princeton, NJ: Princeton University Press.

Basu, K., Bell, C. and Bose, P., 2000, "Interlinkage, Limited Liability and Strategic Interaction", *Journal of Economic Behavior & Organization*, 42: 445–62.

Bates, R., 1981, *Markets and States in Tropical Africa*. Berkeley: University of California Press.

Bell, C., 1988, "Credit Markets and Interlinked Transactions", in H. Chenery and T. N. Srinivasan (eds), *Handbook of Development Economics* 1. Amsterdam: North-Holland.

Bell, C. and Srinivasan, T. N., 1989, "Some Aspects of Linked Product and Credit Market Contracts among Risk-neutral Agents", in Pranab Bardhan (ed.), *The Economic Theory of Agrarian Institutions*. Oxford: Oxford University Press.

Bell, C. and Zusman, P., 1976, "A Bargaining Theoretic Approach to Crop-sharing Contracts", *American Economic Review*, 66: 578–88.

Bell, C., Srinivasan, T. N. and Udry, C., 1997, "Rationing, Spillover, and Interlinking in Credit Markets: The Case of Rural Punjab", *Oxford Economic Papers*, New Series, 49(4): 557–85.

Bhaduri, A., 1973, "A Study in Agricultural Backwardness under Semi-Feudalism", *Economic Journal*, 83(329): 120–37.

Bolton, P. and Dewatripont, M., 2005, *Contract Theory*. Cambridge, MA: MIT Press.

Braverman, A. and Stiglitz, J., 1982, "Sharecropping and the Interlinking of Agrarian Markets", *American Economic Review*, 72(4): 695–715.

Braverman, A. and Stiglitz, J., 1986, "Landlords, Tenants and Technological Innovations", *Journal of Development Economics*, 23: 313–32.

Braverman, A. and Stiglitz, J., 1989, "Credit Rationing, Tenancy, Productivity, and the Dynamics of Inequality", in Pranab Bardhan (ed.), *The Economic Theory of Agrarian Institutions*. Oxford: Oxford University Press.

Brooks, Ray and Ran Tao, 2003, "China's Labor Market Performance and Challenges", IMF Working Paper, November.

Byrd, William and Gelb, Alan, 1990, "Why Industrialize? The Incentives for Rural Community Governments", in William Byrd and Lin Qingsong (eds), *China's Rural Industry: Structure, Development and Reform*. Oxford: Oxford University Press.

Chang, Ha-Joon, 2002, *Kicking Away the Ladder: Development Strategy in Historical Perspective*. London: Anthem Press.

Chao, Kang, 2006, *Essays on the Development of Chinese Cities* (in Chinese). Xinxing Publishing House.

Che, J. and Qian, Y., 1998, "Insecure Property Rights and Government Ownership of Firms", *Quarterly Journal of Economics*, 113(2): 467–96.

Chen, Jianbo, 1995, "The Property Rights Structure and Its Effects on Resource Allocation", *Economic Research Journal*, 9: 24–32.

Chen, Yehua and Zhuo, Xian, 2006, "Cost of Chinese Gradualist Reform and Financial Restructuring of State Banks", *Economic Research Journal* (Jingji Yanjiu), No. 3.

Chen, Z., Wan, G. and Lu, M., 2010, "Inter-industry Income Inequality: An Increasingly Important Cause of the Income Disparity in Urban China – Regression-based Decomposition" (in Chinese), *China Social Sciences*, 3: 6576.

China's Private Sector: Present, Problems and Prospect (a report), 1989, China Social Science Press (Zhongguo Shehui Kexue Chubanshe).

Coase, Ronald, 1937, "The Theory of the Firm", *Economica*, 4(16): 386–405.

Development Research Center of State Council, 2005, "A Survey on the Restructuring of the SOEs", *Property Rights Markets* (Chanquan Shichang), No. 1.

Dewatripont, M. and Maskin, E., 1995, "Credit and Efficiency in Centralized and Decentralized Economies", *Review of Economic Studies*, 62(4): 541–55.

Dixit, Avanish, 2003, "Trade Expansion and Contract Enforcement", *Journal of Political Economy*, 111(6): 1293–317.

Eads, G. and Yamamura, K., 1987, "The Future of Industrial Policy", in K. Yamamura and Y. Yasuba (eds), *Political Economy of Japan*, Vol. 1. Palo Alto, CA: Stanford University Press.

Edwards, S., 1993, "Openness, Trade Liberalization, and Growth in Developing Countries", *Journal of Economic Literature*, 31(3): 1358–93.

Engerman, S. and Sokoloff, K., 2000, "History Lessons: Institutions, Factor Endowments, and Paths of Development in the New World", *Journal of Economic Perspectives*, 14(4): 217–32.

Evans, P., 1987, "Class, State, and Dependence in East Asia: Lessons from Latin Americanists", in F. C. Deyo (ed.), *The New Asian Industrialism*. Ithaca, NY and London: Cornell University Press.

Evans, P., 1995, *Embedded Autonomy: States and Industrial Transformation*. Princeton, NJ: Princeton University Press.

Fudenberg, D. and Maskin, E., 1994, "The Folk Theorem with Imperfect Public Information", *Econometrica*, 62(5): 997–1039.

Gerschenkron, A., 1962, *Economic Backwardness in Historical Perspective*. Cambridge, MA: Harvard University Press.

Greenwald, B. and Stiglitz, E., 1986, "Externalities in Economies with Imperfect Information and Incomplete Markets", *Quarterly Journal of Economics*, 101(2): 229–64.

Hu, Biliang and Zheng, Hongliang, 1996, *TVEs and Rural Development in China*. Shanxi Economics Publishing House (Shanxi Jingji Chubanshe).

Johnson, C., 1982, *MITI and the Japanese Miracle*. Stanford, CA: Stanford University Press.

Kaufmann, Daniel, Kraay, Aart and Mastruzzi, Massimo, 2005, "Governance Matters IV: Governance Indicators for 1996–2004", World Bank Policy Research Working Paper 3630. Washington, DC.

Knight, J. and Yueh, L., 2008. "The Role of Social Capital in the Labour Market in China", *Economics of Transition*, 16(3): 389–414.

Kranton, R., 1996, "Reciprocal Exchange: A Self-Sustaining System", *American Economic Review*, 86(4): 830–51.

Kuang, Jiazai, 1999, "Reform of Rural Financial System since 1978: Policy Evolution", *Research in Chinese Economic History* (Zhongguo Jingjishi Yanjiu), No. 1.

Levin, J., 2003, "Relational Incentive Contract", *American Economic Review*, 93(3): 835–57.

Lewis, W. Arthur, 1954, "Economic Development with Unlimited Supplies of Labor", *Manchester School of Economic and Social Studies*, 22: 139–91.

Li, S., 2003, "Relation-based versus Rule-based Governance: An Explanation of the East Asian Miracle and Asian Crisis", *Review of International Economics*, 11(4): 651–73.

Lin, J., 1995, "The Needham Puzzle: Why the Industrial Revolution Did Not Originate in China", *Economic Development and Cultural Change*, 43(2): 269–92.

Lin, J. and Ren, R., 2006, "Growth Model of East Asian Economies Reconsidered", Working Paper, CCER, Peking University.

List, F., 1956 [1841], *National System of Political Economy*. Philadelphia: Lippincott.

Lu, M., Chen, Z. and Wang, Y., 2007, "Divergence and Convergence: A Theory of Chinese Economic History", *Institutional Economics* (Zhidu Jingjixue), June.

Lu, M., Chen, Z. and Yan, J., 2004, "Increasing Return, Development Strategy and Regional Economic Segmentation", *Economic Research Journal* (Jingji Yanjiu), January: 54–64.

Maddison, Angus, 1998, *Chinese Economic Performance in the Long Run*. Paris: OECD.

Maddison, Angus, 2001, *The World Economy: A Millennial Perspective*. Paris: OECD.

Mitra, P., 1983, "A Theory of Interlinked Rural Transactions", *Journal of Public Economics*, 20: 169–91.

Morduch, J. and Sicular, T., 2001, "Risk and Insurance in Transition: Perspectives from Zouping County, China", in M. Aoki and Y. Hayami (eds), *Communities and Markets in Economic Development*. Oxford: Oxford University Press.

Mulligan, C. and Shleifer, A., 2005, "The Extent of the Market and the Supply of Regulation", *Quarterly Journal of Economics*, 120(4): 1445–73.

Myerson, R., 2004, "Justice, Institutions and Multiple Equilibria", Working Paper, University of Chicago.

Noland, M. and Pack, H., 2003, *Industrial Policy in an Era of Globalization*. Washington: Peterson Institute of International Economics.

North, Douglass and Wallis, John, 1986, "Measuring the Transactions Sector in the American Economy", in S. Engerman and R. Gallman (eds), *Long Period Factors in American Economic Growth*. Chicago: University of Chicago Press.

North, Douglass and Wallis, John, 1994, "Integrating Institutional Change and Technical Change in Economic History: A Transaction Cost Approach", *Journal of Institutional and Theoretical Economics*, 150(4): 609–24.

North, Douglass, Wallis, John and Weingast, Barry, 2006, "A Conceptual Framework for Interpreting Recorded Human History", NBER Working Paper 12795.

Oi, Jean, 1999, *Rural China Takes Off: Institutional Foundations of Economic Reform*. Berkeley: University of California Press.

Pang, J., 1997, "The Role of State in East Asian Economic Transformation", in Luo Jinyi and Wang Zhangwei (eds), *Behind the Miracle: Understanding East Asian Modernization* (in Chinese). Hong Kong: Oxford University Press.

Pitt, M. and Putterman, L., 1992, "Employment and Wages in Township, Village and other Rural Enterprises", Mimeo, Brown University.

Polanyi, Carl, 1957, *The Great Transformation: The Political and Economic Origins of Our Time*. Boston: MA: Beacon Press.

Pomeranz, Kenneth, 2000, *The Great Divergence: China, Europe, and the Making of the Modern World Economy*: Princeton, NJ: Princeton University Press.

Poncet, Sandra, 2003, "Measuring Chinese Domestic and International Integration", *China Economic Review*, 14(1): 1–21.

Qian, Y., 1988, "Urban and Rural Household Saving in China", Staff Papers, International Monetary Fund.

Qian, Y., 1994, "A Theory of Shortage in Socialist Economies Based on the Soft Budget Constraint", *American Economic Review*, 84: 145–56.

Qian, Y. and Roland, G., 1998, "Federalism and the Soft Budget Constraint", *American Economic Review*, 88(5): 1143–62.

Qian, Y. and Weingast, B., 1996, "China's Transition to Markets: Market-Preserving Federalism, Chinese Style", *Journal of Policy Reform*, 1: 149–85.

Qian, Y., Roland, G. and Xu, C., 1988, "Coordinating Changes in M-Form and U-Form Organizations", Mimeo, European Center for Advanced Research in Economics and Statistics, Université Libre de Bruxelles.

Qian, Y., Roland, G. and Xu, C., 1999, "Why China's Different from Eastern Europe? Perspectives From Organization Theory", *European Economic Review*, 43(46): 1084–94.

Ray, D. and Sengupta, K., 1989, "Interlinkages and the Pattern of Competition", in Pranab Bardhan (ed.), *The Economic Theory of Agrarian Institutions*. Oxford: Oxford University Press.

Rona-Tas, A., 1994, "The First Shall be Last? Entrepreneurship and Communist Cadres in the Transition from Socialism", *American Journal of Sociology*, 100(1): 40–69.

Sachs, J. , Woo, W. T. and Yang, X., 2000, "Economic Reforms and Constitutional Transition", *Annals of Economics and Finance*, 1(2): 423–79.

Samuelson, Paul, 1954, "Theoretical Note on Trade Problem", *Review of Economics and Statistics*, 46: 145–64.

Sarap, K., 1991, *Interlinked Agrarian Markets in Rural India*. New Delhi: Sage.

Schelling, T., 1960, *Strategy of Conflicts*. Boston, MA: Harvard University Press.

Shi, Anqing, 2006, "Migration in Towns in China, a Tale of Three Provinces: Evidence from Preliminary Tabulations of the 2000 Census", World Bank Policy Research Working Paper 3890, April.

Solow, Robert, 1956, "A Contribution to the Theory of Economic Growth", *Quarterly Journal of Economics*, 70(1): 65–94.

State Council, 2005, *A Survey Report of Restructuring of SOEs in China*.

Stiglitz, J., 1999, "Quis custodiet ipsos custodes? Corporate Governance Failures in the Transition", in Pierre-Alain Muet and J. E. Stiglitz (eds), *Governance, Equity and Global Markets: Proceedings from the Annual Bank Conference on Development Economics in Europe*. Oxford: Oxford University Press.

Stiglitz, J., 2000, "Formal and Informal Institutions", in P. Dasgupta (ed.), *Social Capital: A Multifaceted Perspective*. Washington, DC: World Bank.

Stiglitz, J. and Yusuf, S. (eds), 2001, *Rethinking the East Asian Miracle*. Oxford: Oxford University Press.

Svejnar, J., 1990, "Productive Efficiency and Employment", in William Byrd and Lin Qingsong (eds), *China's Rural Industry: Structure, Development and Reform*. Oxford: Oxford University Press.

Tsai, K., 2002, *Back-Alley Banking: Private Entrepreneurs in China*. Ithaca, NY: Cornell University Press.

Wade, R., 1990, *Governing the Market*. Princeton, NJ: Princeton: Princeton University Press.

Wang, Yongqin, 2005, *Reputation, Commitment and Organizational Forms: A Study on Comparative Institutions*. Shanghai People's Publishing House.

Wang, Yongqin, 2006, "Interlinking Markets, Relational Contract and Economic Transition", *Economic Research Journal* (Jingji Yanjiu), No. 6.

Wang, Yongqin, 2007, "Interlinking Markets, Relational Contract and Economic Transition", *Studies in Regional Development*, 39(1): 161–87.

Wang, Yongqin and Bao, T., 2007, "Interlinked Contract: Where Do We Stand", Working Paper, China Center for Economic Studies (CCES), Fudan University.

Wang, Yongqin and Li, M., 2008, "Unraveling the Chinese Miracle: A Perspective of Interlinked Relational Contract", *Journal of Chinese Political Science*, 13(3): 269–85.

Wang, Yongqin, Zhang, Yan, Zhang, Yuan, Zhao, Chen and Lu, Ming, 2007, "On China's Development Model: The Cost and Benefits of Decentralization Approach to Transition", *Economic Research Journal* (Jingji Yanjiu), No. 1.

Wang,Yuesheng, 2006a, "Changes of Family Structure in Contemporary China", *The Society* (in Chinese), 3: 118–36.

Wang,Yuesheng, 2006b, "An Analysis of the Changes of Family Structure in Contemporary China", *China Social Sciences* (in Chinese), 1: 96–108.

Wang, Yujian, Lu, Xiongwen, Tao, Zhigang, Jiang, Qingyun, Shao, Qifa and Sun, Yimin, 2007, *Retaking Economic Center Stage* (in Chinese). Shanghai: Shanghai People's Publishing House (Shanghai Renmin Chubanshe).

Weitzman, Martin and Xu, Chenggang, 1994, "Chinese Township and Village Enterprises as Vaguely Defined Cooperatives", *Journal of Comparative Economics*, 18: 121–45.

Williamson, Oliver, 1975, *Markets and Hierarchies: Analysis and Antitrust Implications*. New York: The Free Press.

Williamson, Oliver, 1985, *The Economic Institutions of Capitalism: Firms, Markets, Relational Contracting*. New York: The Free Press.

World Bank, 1993, *The East Asian Miracle: Economic Growth and Public Policy*. Washington, DC: World Bank.

World Bank, 2003, *Improving City Competitiveness through the Investment Climate: Ranking 23 Chinese Cities*. Washington, DC: World Bank.

Yang, Xiaokai and Ng, Yew-Kwang, 1993, *Specialization and Economic Organization*. Amsterdam: North-Holland.

Young, Alwyn, 2000, "The Razor's Edge: Distortions and Incremental Reform in the People's Republic of China", *Quarterly Journal of Economics*, 115(4): 1091–135.

Zhang, Jie, 1998, "Financial Support in China's Gradualist Reform", *Economic Research Journal* (Jingji Yanjiu), No. 10.

Zimmer, Z. and Kwong, J., 2003, "Family Size and Support of Older Adults in Urban and Rural China: Current Effects and Future Implications", *Demography*, 40(1): 23–44.

Index

Page numbers in italic refer to figures and tables.

rule of law: authoritarian governments and implementation of 82; economic development and 4, 73; emergence of 83; index 2; Japan 85; need for political transition 85; timing for 4, 91

rule-based contracts: comparison between relational contracts and *26*, 60–1; enforcement 59, 71; information structure 58; loss compensation 28, 41; market extent and division of labor 24; relational contracts replaced by 74; as social games 60

rule-based governance 10, 73; as appropriate 87; market size 31; as self-sustaining 3; transition from relation-based to 26–7

rural cooperative foundations 65

rural credit unions 43, 46, 65, 66

rural sector: care for the elderly 96; household savings *95*; labor market, land price and income distribution 53–4; labor mobility *104*; reform 65–6, 70, 90, 100; role of families in transition 95

Russia: difference of microeconomic governance between China and 24–6; institutional vacuum during transition 101; rule of law index *2*

Russian-style radicalism 9, 10, 11, 61

Sachs, J. 9

salaries: subsistence level 69; township governmental officials 63

Sarap, K. 46

scarce resources: personal connections and 94

Schelling, T. 82

screening: information asymmetry 47–8

search costs 3, 23, 46, 60, 84, 104, 106

securitization: of NPLs 68

self-enforcing constraint 16

self-enforcing relational contracts 10, 101; as an economizing measure 4, 86–7; early stage of economic development 88; radical reforms and destruction of 11, 24; as social games 60, *see also* Pareto improving relational contracts

self-sustaining governance 3, 4

Sengupta, K. 51

separate contracting 46

separate transactions 45

service sector 29, 36, 38

sharecropping tenancy 3, 47, 48–51, 52, 53, 74

shock therapy 24

Sicular, T. 97

simultaneity: of interlinked contracts 44

Singapore 1, *2*, 72

single market relational contracts 11–16, 59

Smith, A. 28

social anomie 102, 106

social capital 26, 70

social consensus: economic growth 84–5

social inequality 92

social interaction 96, 98–9

social justice 106

social networks 94; and income 106; labor mobility and 103–4; marketization and 102–3; role in transition 96–8

social norms 60, 73, 83

social reform 106

social welfare maximization 77

socioeconomic interactions 58, 60

sociopolitical powers: marketization embedded in 106–7

sociopolitical structure: and economic development 31–2

Soft Budget Constraint Theory 9

Solow, R. 28

South Korea 72; assistance to domestic firms 80; democratization 85, 87; economic development and emergence of middle class 85; economic growth and political legitimacy 77; export performance 80; government control of financial sector 79; government intervention, industrial development 78; government–firm relationship 78; growth rate 1; rule of law index *2*

special interest groups 89

specialization: low level *see* missing or incomplete markets

specialized markets: importance of rule-based contracts 41; incompatibility of localism and 106; replacement of interlinked markets 74; unraveling of interlinked and relational institutions 3, *6*, 25, 60, 84, *88*, 104

Srinivasan, T.N. 47

stage theory: government role, in development 74

stage-contingent industrial policies 78

start-up capital 65

state banks 67–8